So, Who Do You Think You Are?

LORETTA CAMERON

Copyright © 2020 Loretta Cameron.

All rights reserved. No part of this book may be reproduced, stored, or transmitted by any means—whether auditory, graphic, mechanical, or electronic—without written permission of the author, except in the case of brief excerpts used in critical articles and reviews. Unauthorized reproduction of any part of this work is illegal and is punishable by law.

ISBN: 978-1-7356-8913-5 (sc)
ISBN: 978-1-7356-8911-1 (hc)
ISBN: 978-1-7356-8912-8 (e)

Library of Congress Control Number: 2020917595

Because of the dynamic nature of the Internet, any web addresses or links contained in this book may have changed since publication and may no longer be valid. The views expressed in this work are solely those of the author and do not necessarily reflect the views of the publisher, and the publisher hereby disclaims any responsibility for them.

Scripture quotations marked KJV are taken from the King James Version.

Scripture quotations marked AMP are taken from the Amplified® Bible, Copyright © 2015 by The Lockman Foundation. Used by permission.

Scripture quotations marked TPT are from The Passion Translation®. Copyright © 2017, 2018 by Passion & Fire Ministries, Inc. Used by permission. All rights reserved. ThePassionTranslation.com.

Scripture quotations marked NKJV are taken from the New King James Version®. Copyright © 1982 by Thomas Nelson. Used by permission. All rights reserved.

Any people depicted in stock imagery provided by Getty Images are models, and such images are being used for illustrative purposes only. Certain stock imagery © Getty Images.

Lulu Publishing Services rev. date: 01/12/2021

To my precious parents, the late William and Annie Ruth Crawford, who taught me to love God through sound wisdom and true love, which influenced my life and fashioned me into the woman I am today.

Thanks also to my spiritual mothers—the late Rozella McKay, Lillie Bell Baker, Lula Mae Johnson, L. T. Nelson, Willie Mae Pounds, Fannie Lyons, Alphonsa Turner, Johnnie Mae Walker, Ruby Jenkins, and so many more who sowed into my life. Deborah Ann Crawford, Diana Jenkins, Sonja Brown, Patricia Bell, Tracy Gibbins, and a host of others have made an indelible imprint on my heart as well.

To the men who spiritually sowed the seed of God's Word in my life: the late Bishop Isaac King Jr., pastor of Pentecostal COGIC; Apostle Frederick K. C. Price, the founder of Crenshaw Christian Center and Ever-Increasing Faith Ministries; and the late Kenneth E. Hagin, founder of Rhema Bible Training Center.

Each of these godly men and women inspired and encouraged me to know God for myself, to trust Him, and to understand the revealed truth of His Word in total commitment. They taught me to live a life that reflects this revelation, understanding that "my speech and my preaching was not with enticing words of man's wisdom, but in demonstration of the Spirit and of power: That my faith should not stand in the wisdom of men, but in the power of God" (1 Corinthians 2:4–5 KJV).

Contents

Acknowledgments..ix
Preface xi

Chapter 1:   A Journey Set in Motion..1
Chapter 2:   God's Original Plan 13
Chapter 3:   The Slithering Lie 23
Chapter 4:   Believe His Word 33
Chapter 5:   Watch Out—It's Alive 37
Chapter 6:   Sharpen Your Sword..53
Chapter 7:   You Know It's According to Your Faith 63
Chapter 8:   No Issues in My Tissues 75
Chapter 9:   Study to be Sturdy...87
Chapter 10: Nakedness 93
Chapter 11: A Flash from the Past.. 101
Chapter 12: She's God's Woman...109

Acknowledgments

The greatest help in the labor that produced and shaped this dedicated work was that of the Holy Spirit's leading. To Derrick Pete at the Writers Circle Meeting, thank you for your instruction, guidance, and encouragement as I developed this book while taking your class.

Vercina Powell and Steve McCoggle, I'm so grateful for the time you set aside to help with setting the manuscript and computer changes that were made. Minister Sonya Brown, Carol Davis, Nell Merida, Annette Howe, and Dr. Elizabeth Studley, I'm so grateful to have you in my life. You all were the backbone that kept the prayer wheels turning during this awesome writing experience and are most likely the reason there is even a finished product. Lulu, thank you for your input in helping with the publication of this work. Last, but most certainly not least, thank you so much to all of the wonderful people who cheered on this work to its completion.

Preface

My desire and intention to know the God of my life and to find out who I was were set in motion and focus in July 1982 when I received four prophetic words from God. I wanted to help at the church during the summer months and be a blessing to the children. I signed up to assist with vacation Bible school to help teach classes and do whatever else needed to be done. I was ministering to the children, and as I was returning from the pulpit area to my seat, there was a yellow brochure on the floor. I stooped down to pick it up, and on the front of it, there was a picture of a black woman wearing a nurse's uniform. She was a missionary who appeared to be standing in Africa.

As I read the brochure, the voice of God said, "This will be you." I heard these words just as clearly as if I were speaking with you. His words were audible and few but comprehensive in scope. I said, "If this is you, God, then You will have to bring it to pass." As Mary did in Luke 2:19, KJV when she heard the angel of the Lord and "pondered the words in her heart," I did too.

I had no idea how God would do it—or His timing—and I did not do anything to make it happen. Who knew it would take a thirty-year journey for the fullness of the manifestation of God's precise words to come to pass? When God spoke these words to me, I was not a nurse, I was not a missionary, and I had never set foot on the continent of Africa. A revelation resonated deeply in my spirit:

> For I know the plans and thoughts that I have for you, says the Lord, plans for peace and well-being

> and not for disaster to give you a future and a hope.
> (Jeremiah 29:11 AMP)

God knows the plans and thoughts He has for us, and the time should come when the revelation of His plan is revealed in you. We must know the intended storyline He has for us.

> Go ahead and make all the plans you want, but it's the Lord who will ultimately direct your steps.
> (Proverbs 16:1 TPT)

The journey that God outlined for me would be a walk of faith. The Holy Spirit guided me to write the story of how the fulfillment was so strategically planned. His directions placed me in the right place at the right time to receive further instructions on the plans and additional steps to take to further the Gospel with signs following His Word.

It would be nice to say that I was special in His sight or that I was God's favorite. No, I'm just a willing vessel who surrendered to the plans and purpose of God. This means laying down your life for Him and trusting Him to lead you down every path you take—even when things are lacking, painful, or fearful. There will be times when it seems unreachable, unbearable, hopeless. This is the time He promises to be there and make a way of escape for you.

Over a thirty-year period, I've learned to trust Him and depend on Him. My prayer for you is that after reading this book, you will develop a trust in God that surpasses all understanding to aid in comprehending the powerful presence that lives within you and that you are in Him. The idea that you are a created being, truly made in God's image and likeness, may seem preposterous to the human mind, but God is simply awaiting your willingness to abide in His truth. Allow Him to manifest His glory in and through you to go forth and accomplish great and mighty things.

CHAPTER 1

A Journey Set in Motion

There are masses of people whom the Bible refers to as "in the way" (Acts 22:4 KJV). This refers to Christians who are believers and followers of Jesus Christ but who struggle with an unanswered question: "Who am I?"

For years, many Christians have been struggling with finding the answer because their focus has mainly been on the physical/natural realm rather than seeking out the true self, the spirit of humankind. We tend not to contemplate the supernatural aspect because of the urge to rely upon what we can see, touch, hear, smell, and taste. Our flesh has battled since the beginning of time, exploring that which cannot be answered in a sensual realm. Our plans to blaze our own trails and pave roads for those who will follow has yet to explain who we are, why we're here, and what we're supposed to be doing in this walk of life.

Growing up, my family went to church, and the Word of God was ministered to us, but at home, there was very little spiritual fruit present. We lived good, clean, and moral lives; there was no swearing or drinking in our home. However, true spiritual insight was lacking, and there were no Bible studies set aside on our weekly calendars except for church on Sunday mornings and Sunday nights.

Thankfully, years later, my mother gave her life to the Lord and began to practice a lifestyle that exemplified the Christian faith. We paid closer attention to Mother's life after she confessed salvation.

We wanted to see how long it would last and how Daddy would react to her new saintly lifestyle. Her lifestyle did change, and the fruit it produced was astonishing.

About five years later, I joined Mother in the faith. Why it took me five more years to make the best decision of my life, I don't know. There are times when we think that we can work things out ourselves, but we only make them worse.

Being new to the faith in God, my only desire was to know Him more. I set my heart to gain spiritual knowledge in God and to learn who I really was. Prior to accepting Him, I was clueless about who God was in my life. I went to church on Sundays, but I never read the Bible to find more insight to increase my understanding. When I look back, I realize this was senseless. My life was being challenged in relationships, and I desperately needed God. If I didn't allow the working of God's supernatural help, life would be questionable for me.

There are relational issues that were sometimes not resolved, but I chose to focus on the things of God. As I grew in Christ and became more aware of Him and His presence, I began to search more in His Word concerning relationships. I searched every scripture on singleness and marriage and thought, *Why continue when things are so terrible?* God would speak to me, and I would listen, but there were times when the carnal self would take charge. It got to a point when I felt like I had to get away for a while, and my youngest sister and I headed west.

After nine months of separation and seeking God for answers, He spoke through a visiting minister at a very large church I attended. He directed me to return home to my husband. The minister's exact words were these: "Someone here has to return to their husband." This word was clear, but how was I supposed to know that he was speaking to me? After all, there were other women there. I had limited knowledge on knowing the voice of the Lord, but for some reason, deep inside, I knew that those words were meant for me.

Each time the minister would say, "Someone has to return home," my three-year-old son would touch me on the leg and say, "Momma, go up there." I'd push his hand away and say, "Be quiet." This happened at least four times, and each time, my response to my son was the same.

The third time he did it, I threatened to whip him if he didn't stop touching me. During the fourth time, I was assured that this was from God. I rose up from my seat and went to the altar. It was then that the minister stopped pacing the pulpit and saying those words because he knew I was the one he was waiting on. I remember he prayed for everyone at the altar. I knew that this was God, but I was not happy with the message given to me.

After the service ended, I exited the church with a broken spirit and headed home to the place God blessed us with only to meet my sister at the door. Her curiosity beamed, and she instantly knew something wasn't right with me. She inquired about my facial expression. She was aware that I did not leave for church in a state of depression.

I set out a fleece to find out if this was truly God speaking through this man. In my spirit, I knew it was, but the fleshly part of me didn't want it to be God. It's amazing how quick we are to listen to our flesh. I had set out with my own plans to never return home and live with someone I could no longer trust.

I had read about Gideon and how he wanted to be sure it was God speaking to him. I asked God for a sign. I said to God, "If this is you, then let something in the form of writing ask me to come home." I knew the benefits of fasting and praying because we would fast every Tuesday and Friday at the church I grew up in. After three days of fasting and spending time in prayer, a handwritten letter addressed to me came in the mail. This really astounded me because God had spoken through His vessel and answered my prayer through fleecing. Wow! For me to say that it was an easy decision to honor what God had spoken through His man of God and the fleecing would be far from the truth. I was so disappointed and upset that God had interrupted my life to alter my plans, but I knew that "obedience is better than sacrifice" (1 Samuel 15:22 KJV), and I obeyed God.

What's Shown Is Not Always Seen

I realized this journey didn't just begin with the fleecing; it began in 1973, before I gave my life to the Lord. God has a way of getting you to the point where you need to be—even if you are "wandering in your wilderness" (Exodus 8:28 KJV).

One of my mother's close friends held a supervisory position, and she hired me to work in her department. During a seven-year period of transferring to three different departments, God directed me to be in the right place at the right time. When I think back on those seven years and three transfers, I realize seven is God's number of spiritual perfections. Three represents wholeness and divine perfection; the Trinity (the Father, the Son, and the Holy Ghost), and "the Spirit, the water, and the blood" (1 John 5:8 KJV). The number three also symbolizes growth and multiplication. It happened during the final transfer from the Dietetics Department to the Surgical Department. The position I accepted in Environmental Services seemed like a step in the wrong direction to some people.

We were a group of five, and our job was to clean the operating rooms after the surgical procedures were completed. During the surgeries, we waited in a closet-sized room. We were not just sitting idle with nothing to do; we were learning the Word of God as we refilled our cleaning supplies.

I was a new Christian, and there was an elderly woman who would bring her Sunday school pamphlets to work. We would all study them and learn the Bible. Two of our team members had an eye for each other during our study time, but they acted like nothing was going on between them. I was very serious about my new life and wanted to learn everything I could about God. I'd take my pamphlets home and teach them to my little son since he was so eager to learn about God.

I knew that cleaning operating rooms for the rest of my life was not my destiny, yet I struggled to find out exactly what it should be. Talking with other people there broadened my vision, and I then searched out other opportunities.

God's timing came one day when we had finished cleaning a room. I was wondering what actually went on in those rooms and what it was like to take part in a surgical procedure. I stood at the door and looked in to see what went on and what I could learn.

As I was looking into that room, someone in nursing education came up behind me and asked if I would like to do that. I turned toward them and said yes.

They immediately went to their office, made a phone call to an inner city college, and spoke with the director. They came back and said, "I've gotten you into the program, which has already begun. The requirement is that you make an A for the first portion of the class to move on in the program."

I assured them that I would make the grade and not be a disappointment. I was given all the necessary information to meet with and speak to the program director.

Was this a coincidence? Absolutely not. It was a divine connection to His plan for me. Little did I know that God had set the stage for an amazing journey in life. I held to the promise I made to pass the class with an A, and I successfully completed the second half of the program. I knew God had opened the door for me. The entire program took a year and a half to complete, and God's blessings enabled me to only take six months of classes with the program. After that, I was hired and trained in the work I had studied for.

I felt honored because the other students had to pay for their clinical training, and I was being paid for my clinical training. I was fortunate to be trained by a well-known, prestigious employer, and I acquired great experience. I received the skills that would catapult me into the plan and purpose that I was to fulfill. It was the beginning of a lifelong encounter through the eyes of faith.

As a younger person, I never set a goal of working in an operating room. I truly believe that this was planned "before I ever came to be" (Jeremiah 1:5 KJV). I was hired in that department as an environmental service aide, and within a very short time, I was chosen to work with maintaining the availability of instruments for the procedures. That happened to be the training ground for the surgical technician position that God supernaturally opened the door to.

Serving God was very profound for me. I had never experienced such wondrous favor, and I did not have the sound knowledge about who He is. I set out to learn who Father God was and how I could get to know Him without thinking to ask for anything. It was important that I increased in the knowledge of God, realizing that once I established a relationship with Him, my life was going to be an exciting, thrilling, and fulfilling adventure both naturally and supernaturally. Being a new believer, a babe in Christ, and seeing things happen so fast was mind-boggling to me, and it deepened my desire to worship God more intimately.

Finding Pieces That Fit

This renewed life in Christ was sort of like a jigsaw puzzle. I was wondering how the pieces would all fit together. While all of the steps of putting a puzzle together are challenging, it all begins with building upon one piece. My one piece was accepting the plan of salvation in Jesus Christ. At the time, some people who were closely connected to me made fun of my walk with the Lord by calling me "Holier than Thou." The words were painful because I never thought of myself as being holier than anyone else. I just wanted to please the Lord. Being bothered by the words from those close to me only increased my faith to trust and believe that nothing is impossible with God and that I would weather this storm.

It was a constant thing with some who did not and could not understand my new way of thinking and living. Not long after, I decided to not even consider what was being said anymore.:

> But the natural man receives not the things of the Spirit of God: for they are foolishness unto him: neither can he know them, because they are spiritually discerned. (1 Corinthians 2:14 KJV).

This scripture helped me learn how to deal with unbelievers who were seemingly sent just to cause aggravation in my life and to try to deter me from the godly path of purpose and destiny. When the hurt comes from those you love dearly, the pain seems to intensify. All sorts of thoughts came into my mind. At times, I wanted to respond directly to their comments in the flesh of carnality, "but thanks be unto God" (1 Corinthians 15:57 KJV). He abides on the inside of us and helps our spirits remain in charge so we can do the right thing.

As I continued choosing the ways of God by reading and studying at every opportunity, my spirit man began to flourish. I became more settled and grounded. I no longer reacted emotionally to the nasty comments that were being said. I had learned how to bring my body under subjection and allow the words to roll right on by and never again stop in my mind for processing. When we buy into the negative, we become frustrated and angry. Instead of reminiscing about what had been said, I learned to quote scripture for what God said about me.

I learned that the Word of God works when we apply it directly to the situation. As I began to see the changes in myself, I no longer worried about what others thought. I became more in touch with me. I experienced a spiritual transformation. I was no longer a perplexed, timid person with low self-esteem. I was gradually developing into the godly woman I was originated to be.

The hunger and thirst for more of God escalated to the point that all I desired to do was feed my spirit man. For a very long time, I couldn't see my kitchen table because it was filled with all kinds of different translations of the Bible, commentaries, dictionaries, notes, and notebooks. I felt the need to be a part of every worship service.

Praying with the church mothers was a special time because these women were serious about getting ahold of God, seeking His face, and receiving answers to their prayers. I learned that prayer service is the power source for the church. It is the catalyst that guided the manifestation of God's presence, and souls were saved. That's when people were walking to the altar to meet with God. They did not care who was looking, and they knew that the need to be transformed by the power of God was real.

Learning to pray and how to pray was truly a game changer for me. My brother rarely went to church, but he was there one Sunday. The pastor preached a powerful word, and my brother turned to me and said, "Did Momma tell him anything about me?"

I responded, "I don't think so." I explained that God knows everything about us and how the move of the Holy Spirit was leading in the message. I wanted my brother to give his life over to the Lord that day, but it didn't happen. However, that did not stop me from continuing on in faith. I believed and knew that he would one day accept Jesus into his heart and receive the salvation that had already been provided for him before the beginning of time. Through consistent prayer and faith in what I was believing God for, my brother eventually gave his life to the Lord before his departure from time into eternity.

I could see the blessings manifesting in my life, but I did not fully understand why or the path it was taking me on. I did not know that this missionary expedition would include the medical field, the world of nursing, and third world countries. A humble young lady who decides to follow God's lead would endeavor upon a journey that would open doors to spiritually minister to doctors, nurses, technicians, and other professionals throughout the country. The presence of His glory led the way for miracles to happen right before their eyes. It would change the hearts and minds of so many who were searching for God without knowing how to reach Him. I met thousands of people who were open to teachings about God, spiritual principles, studying the Word of God, and learning to listen to and live the Christian way through faith, love, and wisdom by the Spirit of God.

For years, God's presence in my life continued to increase with powerful anointings that literally destroyed yokes. It's so amazing when we read about how God used others in the faith to operate in His power, but it's an explosive supernatural experience when He uses you. Many people have heard about God, there are many people who simply know about God, and a few people have experienced the power of God in their lives.

There is an accountability with the power of God being evident in our lives. It's not something that we plug into when we have a need for His intervention. It is not like when we need to use an appliance or electronic equipment. We must remain plugged in and tuned in to His Spirit for guidance. There is a lifestyle of commitment to being and doing what God has called us to and ordained us to be.

Too often, we see others being used by God—and we desire the same thing. Are we willing to do what they have done to get to that place in Him? Are we willing to deny ourselves and lay down our lives for the promises He's given? I ask these questions because there is a price to be paid that the flesh doesn't want to employ.

The Leading of His Spirit: When He Leads, Just Follow

> For all who are led by the Spirit of God are the sons of God.
> —Romans 8:14 KJV

Being led denotes a following, and the one you follow should have already been proven as a leader. My decision to yield to the Spirit of God was the best decision of my life. It was as if I sprouted the wings of a wren and rapidly developed the wings of an eagle. The wingspan of an eagle is around six to eight feet, and its size is relative to a six-foot man. Spiritual growth brings physical growth and maturity.

In each stage of life, we must do things to receive our intended results. Physical growth requires exercises that must happen in order to shape the body in the way we desire. There are times when we have to do things that are not comfortable or that cause pain or muscle aches. Exercise is an activity that most people do not want to engage in, but many of them desire the body of someone who does. They've seen the results, but they lack the vigor to reach the goal.

We tend to think that things just happen without our participation. Want a revelation? It doesn't! You have to take part in life to get what you desire. It takes a commitment to the gym for the workout to be successful. The body is sort of like dough; you can mold it and shape it to your liking, but it takes work. We can't eat all the food we see, never exercise, lead sedentary lifestyles, and simply believe that our faith will get us to the place we want to be.

The same principle applies spiritually when we're committed to the challenge of a desired goal. Yes, Christians desire to know God intimately and establish a close-knit relationship with God. Jesus said, "No man is able to pluck you out of my Father's hand" (John 10:29 KJV). Right after He spoke these words, he said, "I and My Father are one" (John 10:30 KJV). It is truly His desire that we become one with Him.

God's desire for His creation is that we come to know Him as the only true and living God. This is why He gave us eternal life by revealing the "word of His power" (Hebrews 1:3 KJV). God's righteousness working in us enables one to live a lifestyle of holiness through faithfulness, prayer, and the commitment that we receive all that He has for us in this life. Oops! Did I say holiness? Yes, I did. God is just as powerful now as He was when we first come to know Him—and He always will be.

As I developed this relationship with Him, I began to see the power of His Spirit. I experienced His presence on a larger scale than I had ever dreamed was possible. As I encountered others, an opportunity presented itself. The Lord show Himself mightily through His Word, a prayer, or a simple touch, and true relationships were established.

I clearly heard the voice of God say, "This will be you."

I responded, "God, if this is You, then You will have to bring it to pass." This was a rhema word because it was spoken to me through the mouth of God during a time when I just wanted to be a blessing to my pastor and help the children learn about the One who created them to live life to the fullest with the guidance of the Holy Spirit. I did not tell anyone what I heard in the sanctuary that day. I wasn't led to share it with my pastor or my mother at the time. With the assurance that I knew what I heard was real, it was interesting to see how and when He would carry out His plan for me.

These few words from God changed my entire life and gave me brand-new sight that would come from within rather than seeing with the natural eye. This inner renewal of my spirit was as if the heavens were parted and the glory of the Lord was draped over me. I knew with all my heart that He was about to do something in me that was much larger than I was. Since I didn't have clear direction about the steps to take, it was a total walk of faith.

God will make impressions in your inner man that set off a knowing as to where you should be, what you should say, and to whom you should say it. He'll lead you to the place where the blessings are. The people you will encounter are waiting for your arrival.

Standing at the door of the operating room and looking in with no intention other than seeing what goes on in a surgical suite was the first step in the plan to reach the people who God had in His heart to bless. The search for more of God's presence intensified, which helped me understand how the Word of God actually works. I learned that His Word is alive, it is quick, and it is powerful, and I wanted to know if what was written was truly so.

The Word of God was my priority, and I wanted to know what God's original intention was for humanity to live upon the earth. Was it possible to regain the original plan that was established in His Word? Did the restoration through the blood of Jesus provide a pathway to recover that which was lost with the entry of sin?

We must be as tenacious as the people from Berea:

> These were more noble than those in Thessalonica, in that they received the word with all readiness of mind, and searched the scriptures daily, whether those things were so. (Acts 17:11 KJV)

I set out on a path to find out how to enter the powerful realm of God through faith, obedience, and total reliance upon Him.

CHAPTER 2

God's Original Plan

Adam, the first man created by God, breathed the breath of life and became a spirited being with infinite potential. God formed man out of the dust of the earth:

> And the Lord God formed man of the dust of the ground and breathed into his nostrils the breath of life; and man became a living soul. (Genesis 2:7 KJV)

Science has discovered that the same minerals and elements in the ground are found in the human body. The body's composition includes oxygen, carbon dioxide, hydrogen, nitrogen, calcium, phosphate, iron, sodium, chloride, and magnesium. Since these minerals and elements are found in the earth's soil, why is there any question about how humans were formed and by whom?

The Creator of all things pertaining to life is the subject of the creation versus evolution discussion among those to who think there is no Supreme Being. This scripture explains how man was created, in whose image he was created, and why man was created.

> And God said, "Let us make man in our image, after our likeness: and let them have dominion over the fish of the sea, the fowl of the air, and over the cattle and over all the Earth, and over every creeping thing that

crept upon the earth." So, God created man in his own image. In the image of God created he them: male and female he created them. (Genesis 1:26–27 KJV)

These verses assure us that God intended for man to be revealed in the earth realm just as He is revealed in heaven. On several occasions, the Bible says, "And God said" (Genesis 1:3 KJV). This ensured that what was spoken by God the Father, the Creator of all things, will only result in the inevitable when His principles are applied.

Now, let's take a look to what He said. "Let's make man in our image" (Genesis 1:26 KJV). This image is the representation of an external form, person, or thing. When using a camera, we take pictures of an object, and when we look at them, the picture is an exact image of what we've seen. When the Master of creation created us, He used his own image to bring it to pass so that we would be exactly as He is. God stamped His image in us and upon us. It is to be understood that we are spirit beings with souls and live in bodies. Adam represents humankind on earth. God has the same power of authority and ability to operate here on earth as He does in heaven. This authority was given to Adam when God gave him dominion.

Once we realize that the power of heaven abides in our spirit, we will operate in the dominion of His power. Think about this for a moment: "dominion over all the earth." God gave Adam ruling power, authority, and control over every situation. God empowered Adam with the dominance and command over every region, territory, province, state, and colony. He was given authority over all the earth.

When we think about genetics, it represents the property of a gene of an offspring from a parent. Spiritually, this is what happened to every created being and child of the Living God. He imparted the very expression of His Spirit in Adam to do His will and operate in Him—but never apart from Him. God's Word to Adam in the Garden of Eden was meant for every seed that would stem from him being fruitful and multiplying.

God's Word is powerfully packaged, and every "shall" of His is loaded. We are truly a reflective image of Who He is in the earth. Just as life began at conception, and the offspring takes on the genetic attributes of the parent, so it is with the Father of Life when Adam was created in His likeness. He created spiritual copies of Himself in the form of human beings to represent Him on earth. If we only believe that we are speaking spirits housed in bodies, placed in a tangible world to operate on a spiritual level, our communities and surrounding areas would not be spiritually deprived.

Adam had every intention of carrying out God's plan until other influences captured his attention. Adam was given an awesome responsibility and leadership role in the formation of the future of spirited beings. His innocence is sometimes mistaken for the thought of him being created with perfection. Adam was a created man just as every other person is—with the exception of being formed from the earth by God and being given the first breath of life with a supernatural experience.

Adam was never intended to be a robot or be controlled; he was created with the power of choice. He was allowed to make choices after the One who created him gave the instructions. Yes, the One who named all of the animals, commissioned to be "fruitful and multiply, subdue the earth and fill it, rule over the fowls of the air, fish of the sea, over the cattle of the field, and every living thing that moves upon the earth, given every yielding seed, plant, and tree for food" (Genesis 1:28 KJV). With everything supplied and promised, Adam was distracted by outside influences.

Adam's attention was diverted from what he was promised and given to what he thought sounded better, appeared to look better, or seemed better in the moment. With creation being completed and God's stamp of approval on His work, the earth was ready to be influenced and populated with beings that were supposed to love and fellowship with Him throughout eternity.

The initial strategic supernatural plan was to "make man in our own image, in our likeness" (Genesis 1:26 KJV). Now, what could that have meant? I believe it is the resemblance, similitude, and expression of who God is in the spiritual realm manifested on earth. His desire is for someone to speak His Word and call things into existence, command the storm to cease, and operate with kingdom authority over the seas, the air, the beast of the field, and everything that creeps upon the earth.

Adam's eyes were spiritually open to know that he was created in the image of God and in his likeness. Adam experienced God's presence every day: "They heard the voice of the Lord God walking in the garden in the cool of the day" (Genesis 3:8 KJV). This could have not been the first time He came because Adam recognized his voice in the Garden of Eden and hid.

In Genesis 1:28 God clearly spoke blessings and commissioned them to be fruitful, to multiply, to replenish, to subdue, and to have dominion. Studying this verse should empower people to excel far beyond their human abilities. To be fruitful (*Parah*) means to bear fruit, be fruitful, and branch off, to grow, to increase (Touch Loaded Bible). God's design in creating a man and a woman had a purpose: to procreate the fabulous union of two becoming one. It was for Adam to produce more with great results—a prolific breeding of offspring that would bring praise and glory to the heavenly Father. Without His creation, none would exist. It's God's desire that fruitfulness is engraved in the hearts and minds of all individuals.

To communicate His established plan throughout generations to come, Jesus often taught of "being fruitful, producing good fruit, corrupt fruit, evil fruit, fruit of the Vine, and those yielding no fruit" (Matthew 3:10 KJV). The subject is well addressed in the New Testament, which will be discussed in later chapters.

Multiplication generates thoughts of growth, things being duplicated, escalating, with rapid increase. God's plan for Adam was to experience this type of multiplication in whatever he put his hands on. God expected Adam to increase in every arena—his leadership in family matters, tilling the grounds, and keeping the Garden of Eden—of responsibility given him. In marriage, when the two become one, multiplication erupts sometimes in a single birth, twins, triplets, quadruplets, sextuplets, and sometimes more; that's an increase. In the same way, every sphere of our lives can and will multiply if we adhere to godly principles of lifestyle ordained by the Father of light.

God spoke compelling words to Adam in positioning him to fulfill his purpose and destiny. Adam was commissioned to *replenish* the earth and not just a small region. The task at hand to the finite mind would cause one to think it might be impossible. People might question how and where to begin. This command was given to him before the fall of humanity; all things were in his care, and the supply exceeded the demand. With one other person, every tree bearing fruit after its kind restoring, refilling, and replacing is imminent.

Just as God spoke the Word, and it was so, Adam was created with the same ability and spiritual insight. Provision to replace and recover what was used is satisfied in the storehouse of God. Whatever has been depleted—spiritually, mentally, physically, or emotionally—is to be returned, restored, reestablished, reinstated, refilled, renewed, redeemed, refreshed, and made up to you. This is why David so boldly said, "The Lord is my Shepherd and I shall not want!" (Psalm 23:1 KJV).

There are proprietary rights in ownership. The earth and the fullness thereof belong to our heavenly Father, and as heirs of God and joint heirs with Christ Jesus, there is a covenant right to whatever is needed at whatever time it is supplied. The Shepherd supplies the need for the sheep. Taking hold of what's been given you through faith commands results.

When God commissioned Adam to *subdue*, it was a more personal intent, and once mastered, he operated on a level to even greater extent. Thoughts of subduing bring to mind conquering, bringing things into subjection, discipline, or forcefulness. Had Adam tamed the fleshly soul's desire to know good and evil, maybe the fall of humanity would not have occurred. Subduing the craving and wants of the flesh must be subjugated or subservient to the will of the Spirit. God has given everything needed in life to pursue our assignments and walk in victory.

There are times when force is needed and must be instrumental in accomplishing one's goals. In life, we can simply soften a thing with less intensity. Bring the self under godly submission and control with the help of the Holy Spirit. Be led by the Holy Spirit. Adam made the right choices until he was temped with fleshly desire to know more.

God gave instruction to *dominate* in life:

> And God said, Let us make man in our image, after our likeness: and let them have dominion over the fish of the sea, and over the fowl of the air, and over the cattle, and over all the earth, and over every creeping thing that crept upon the earth. (Genesis 1:26 KJV)

That covers it all: dominion in every aspect of life, operating within a sphere of influence where you dominate, and ruling in power and authority.

This authority is given to all who will submit and believe, male or female. The Lord gave this commission to both Adam and Eve. He blessed them, and then released them to operate in it. He made a final assessment and saw everything. "It was very good" (Genesis 1:31 KJV).

While Adam gave names to the animal kingdom being male and female, there was no other human who would complement him. Adam was put to sleep by God, the first anesthesiologist, and then He removed a rib from his side, the first thoracic surgeon.

> And the rib, which the Lord God had taken from man, made he a woman, and brought her unto the man. (Genesis 2:22 KJV)

The first pathologist took the specimen, diagnosed it, and created a woman. That's the first plastic surgeon. Science is all throughout the Word of God, and if we search the scriptures, our doubts and fears will be eradicated.

God brought the woman to Adam, and upon gazing her beauty, Adam was overwhelmed in his emotions: "She shall be called Woman, because she was taken out of man" (Genesis 2:23 KJV).

God's plan will forever exceed human plans. The woman was created after God had established all that Adam would need in order to fulfill his purpose. Adam was settled in position before the woman became a living soul. He had daily work, he had a place to reside, and he had surplus.

Women, there is wisdom to learn from Adam's story. Adam was given a wife after the foundation was built. God, seeing His work complete, brought to Adam all the animals he formed from the ground to see what Adam would call them. One brilliant mind operating at great magnitude in naming all of God's created beast, fowl, and sea creatures, but he had no name for the woman created for him. Everything God does is with purpose.

It's in Her Name

Creation of the woman was to assist in bringing forth life in the fulfillment of what was spoken to them. Adam couldn't do it alone; he needed a helpmate who would receive a deposited seed and eventually bring forth another living soul to multiply and replenish the earth. It was God's plan to create the woman. God was planning for Adam's and every other man's future to be filled with adulation, completion, and assistance.

The woman God gave to Adam was positioned to give life. She would complement and work side by side with him, being symbolic of the Holy Spirit. In John 14:16 (KJV), Jesus prayed, "The Father, and he shall give you another Comforter, that he may abide with you forever." The "Comforter" refers to the Holy Spirit, and the Greek word for comforter is *paracletes*, which means "one summoned or called to one's side, one called alongside to help" (Loaded Touch Bible). A comforter is called to one's aid.

Up until Adam fell, she was only referred to as "the woman." She had no identity as to who she really was. When she was given a name, her identity was revealed. When things are in disarray, restoration is imminent. The beguiling deception of the woman by the serpent—along with her influence upon Adam in giving him the fruit to eat—caused spiritual devastation that affected the entire world God created. Their innocence was shattered, their vision was lost, their purpose was deferred, and their nakedness was revealed. The disobedience of God's command cost them the intended spiritual life of promise: "Ye shall not eat of it neither shall ye touch it" (Genesis 3:3 KJV).

She failed to realize that touching the tree wouldn't make her wise because she was created from wisdom, in wisdom, and with wisdom. The serpent deceived her into thinking that if she ate from this forbidden tree, the fruit would make her like God. She must have forgotten that she was already like God, being created in His image and in His likeness. He's the only wise, true, and living God. Every attribute in Him was in them. This is much of what professing Christians are operating in today, thinking, *If I could only be like God.* You already are; you're created to look and act exactly like Him.

Eating the fruit only brought devastation and shame upon

what was once going to be paradise for life. Questioned by God about Adam's location was simply rhetorical. God is omniscient; he knows all things. Adam and the woman hid behind fig leaves to cover up what had been exposed. They each came to envisage seeing generations of sin throughout the world they were created to replenish. As Adam and his wife tried to conceal their fallen state, God said, "Who told thee that thou were naked? Have you eaten from the tree whereof I commanded thee that thou shouldest not eat?" (Genesis 3:11 KJV).

God addressed Adam—and not the woman. The command was given to the man whom he placed in the Garden "to dress it and to keep it" (Genesis 2:15 KJV). God's order was that the man was to work and labor in serving to maintain and retain that which was given him, holding as his own. The Garden of Eden belonged to him. Once Adam tasted the forbidden fruit, sin entered. However, nothing supervened when the woman first ate of the fruit. God questioned the man, and he blames God and the woman rather than taking ownership of his desire to commit treason by violating God's ordinance.

He was given complete authority over everything that crept upon the ground, including serpents. Adam replied, "The woman whom thou gave to be with me, she gave me of the tree, and I did eat" (Genesis 3:12 KJV). The authority given has to be initiated to defeat the enemy. Adam, in attendance with Satan and the woman's enticing conversation, refused to take charge of a compromising and unfavorable plight, abandoning his rule and reign over the earth. Everything was privilege to Adam in fulfilling his purpose in obtaining that which God had prepared for him; his destiny was temporarily relinquished into the hand of Satan.

At that point, Adam needed restoration to his rightful place, desiring to be redeemed from decisions he'd made, looking to be renewed in his spirit, comforted by a love one, and made to feel alive again. God expects a man to walk in the authority he's given, follow instructions, be unyielding, and be impenetrable to any circumstance he finds himself experiencing. God is, and always will be, our Source.

Because he "harkened to the voice of his wife," (Genesis 3:17 KJV), God cursed the serpent and the ground and multiplied sorrow upon the woman in childbirth with desire to her husband. He is now to rule over her. This turning point of life has become a grievously moral encounter. Life outside of the ark of God tends to leave us uncovered and exposed to the enemy's territory. After the fall from grace, the woman was given a name. Adam named her Eve because "she was the mother of all living things" (Genesis 3:30 KJV). She would now be the one to stroke his ego, help build his masculinity, restore his leadership role by being in submission to him, and help allocate the parameters of obedience in living the promise.

She now must live her name by bringing life to whatever situations her family may encounter. Her initial role was to complement her husband in which they both were given ownership of authority with dominion to rule, and now she is to desire him above all other things, only second to God. Being the mother of all living things, she's the carrier to reproduce what God created: life. Naturally and spiritually, her life was where the anointing was placed on the inside of her. God created the woman to bring forth life in every sphere. Women, take note. We must carry out the intended plan of God.

The Garden of Eden was a place of exotic beauty, a place of rest, a place of plentiful resources, a place of pure joy, a place where faithful promises originated, a taste of heaven on earth, and God's paradise for his created beings. God created every tree for food to nourish the body was provided and every herb and plant of the field before it reached the earth. It never rained upon the earth, for God had the mist of the dew from the earth to irrigate the land. An ever-loving Father would provide all that was needed to live upon the land. The beauty of the landscape was a wonder to gaze upon: good, nourishing food, unending orchards of every fruit known to humanity, the tree of life, in the midst of the garden, and the tree of knowledge of good and evil.

These two determining factors would change the course of life for humankind. Freedom of choice is a powerful responsibility when there is a war among your members. The flesh is constantly challenged in opposition to the spirit. The very thing God says not to touch suddenly becomes the focus of what you desire to touch and know. Realizing there are consequences to our actions, we tend to think we know more than our Creator. "Thou shalt not surely die" (Genesis 3:3 KJV). The deception of the lie seems to have hope of having it both ways. Did Eve know that spiritual disaster was at the door?

The River of Eden flowed out to water the garden, and at a certain point, it streamed into four directions to encompass the entire land. The first river, Pison, describes the location of the Garden of Eden. The Hebrew meaning of Pison is "increase," and the Bible says that gold, bdellium, and onyx stone is found there. The second river, Gihon, or "bursting forth," is a spring near Jerusalem where the anointing and proclaiming of Solomon as king took place. It encompasses the entire land of Ethiopia. The third river, Hiddekel, or "rapid," coursed east toward Assyria, which is also known as Tigris. The fourth river, Euphrates, "to break forth, rushing, fruitfulness, is the largest and longest river in western Asia. It rises from two chief sources in the Armenian mountains and flows into the Persian Gulf (Loaded Bible Genesis 2:10–15).

The body of water surrounding the garden in which Adam was to take care of was speaking prophetically to him each time he looked out upon the waters. The Pison was speaking *increase* to him. God is making him greater in the number of resources of gold and precious stone in strength, size, and territory. The earth belonged to them. The *Gihon* was saying, "You will be *bursting forth* on every end. Things in your life shall overflow, and you shall possess an overwhelming quantity and quality of surplus." The Hiddekel speaks of the sudden, *rapid* growth of the blessings and the swiftness and immediate access to whatever the need is. The Euphrates speaks of the blessing's progression. With rapid acceleration, it speaks forth what is commanded.

How great is our God? The river transforms and flows from the Word of God. Let's put that in common language: God desired an abundant supply that would be visibly bursting forth at the seam with the promptness of its manifestation in speaking His Word.

Paradise was sculpted and designed by God for both to spend a life wanting and lacking nothing. Adam was given a place there to dress and keep the garden with instructions for living an abundant life. Eve's position was to replenish life in the flesh through the gifting of her reproductive assets. Who would want to mess that up?

God's plan shall forever trump ours. Every time we miss it, He is there with the redemptive plan to reroute our paths.

CHAPTER 3

The Slithering Lie

The Fall, Questioning God

The fall of man was devised by an enemy whose initial plans were to "ascend in the heavens, exalt his throne above the stars of God: sit also upon the mount of the congregation, in the sides of the north. Ascend above the heights of the clouds; and be like the Most High" (Isaiah 14:13–14 KJV).

Lucifer, as he was known before his abrupt departure from the heavens, was sure he could undermine the Ancient of Days to gain access to the throne. What he deemed to be an elaborate plan to defeat the Lord of the heavens landed him an eternal destination of fire and brimstone. The Bible says, "Yet thou shalt be brought down to hell, to the sides of the pit" (Isaiah 14:15 KJV). A created being thinking He is greater than the One who caused him to be? What catastrophic thinking to plan his own demise!

Lucifer, an angelic spirited being, excelled with worship. We can only imagine what it was like being the first spirit virtuoso leading the praise and worship of the heavens. He was given this name meaning "light bearer," which is who he was until pride set in and the urge to be great or greater than the One who created him. He was a shining light among the stars of heaven and inclined to worship around the throne and the angels. There are "six things that are detestable to God and seven are an abomination to him" (Proverbs 6:16 KJV). Pride leads the list.

Lucifer developed an inordinate opinion of himself to believe that he was privileged to exalt himself. He believed he could pull rank on the Lord of lords. He wanted the praise and glory that was, is, and will always belong to the Father. God said, "I am the Lord; that is my name! I will not give My Glory to another, neither My Praise to graven images" (Isaiah 42:8 KJV). What was Lucifer thinking? He was not God, and he had not created anything except for the foolishness in his mind. Just as it is today, we tend to think we can exalt ourselves to places and positions that God has not called us to.

Pride is subtle and creeps into the spirit cunningly. They act as if they are superior to others because they have been given a title. As soon as you have elevated yourself, you no longer have a heart for souls; you now have a heart to control. God never desires for us to control anyone except ourselves. He created us with the power to choose. If anyone had authority to control others, it truly would be Him, but He chose not to.

He gave us dominion over everything except one another, and we find in most places of worship, leadership with crab mentality that mimics worldly operations. They step on and over everyone else to get into a certain posture that will enhance and reveal their pride. They are jockeying for position because most believers really are not sure who they are, where God wants to take them, or what their life assignments are.

Many Christians lose faith, quit the church, and refuse to forgive because someone has hurt them. "I used to bring the pastor water, but now Sister So-in-so is doing it—and they didn't say anything to me about not doing it." "I was the pastor's right hand, and now so-in-so seems to be doing what they want to because the pastor put them in my place." Petty, petty, petty. The enemy wants to see division among the saints. Just know you have been given a position.

> And hath raised us up together and made us to sit together in heavenly places in Christ Jesus: That in the ages to come he might show the exceeding riches of his grace in his kindness toward us through Christ Jesus. (Ephesians 2:6–7 KJV)

God displayed you in the spiritual realm, being seated in Christ Jesus, and its manifestation in the natural realm transcends human limitations that cause you to rise above the pain and being overlooked and bypassed.

Just know, without a doubt, that we did not earn this salvation. The authority that operates in you came about through Christ's death on the cross. He positioned you in the heavenly place, and it is by the grace of God that you're redeemed. No one can remove you from the station God has called you to but you. Christ paid it all, and when we choose to exalt ourselves, we will be made low.

The serpent is a subtler creation than the other beast of the field that God created (Genesis 3:1 KJV). Satan's scheme had no effect, and he was disbarred from the heavens. Jesus said to the seventy, "I beheld Satan fall as lightning fall from heaven" (Luke 10:18 KJV).

God alleviated the situation with swiftness; it was so fast that Jesus describes it "as lightning." It was faster than a flash. We describe lightning as a flash. God has no desire for the enemy to get ahead with anything, and that should be the mind-set of his creation: every living breathing person on the face of this earth.

Like Eve, the believer will play patty-cake with the enemy by giving an ear to listen to the lies. She knew what God had said and what the order of the day was. She allowed him to persuade her into thinking, *What if I taste it? What if I can be like God? What will happen if I am made to be wiser than I already am?* As wise as she was, she never thought to think things through alone the lines of the truth that resided in her.

This was not the first time she looked upon a snake. None of the other reptiles spoke to her in the Bible. She should have realized that the snake was talking and thought, *What kind of snake is this?* Satan embodied the serpent and began to lie to the woman God created. She tuned in to a conversation that she should have not addressed with any other words except to say, "I know what God has said." She should have abruptly ended the conversation. That is working the Word of God. We cast the devil out with the scriptures.

"And no marvel; for Satan himself is transformed into an angel of light" (2 Corinthians 11:14 KJV). The Amplified version says, "And no wonder, since Satan masquerades as an angel of light." I believe this translation says it well: masquerading. Satan is full of disguises and façades. The Bible is clear on this, yet believers remain prey to the deceitfulness of Satan. He has gotten a little cleverer with his lies and uses the one weapon he has under false pretense. What the serpent did to Eve with the influence of satanic control was to get her to doubt what she knew to be the truth. His weapon is used to this day, and the only reason he is somewhat effective using it is that most believers have not studied the manual that contains all the promises that are *yes* and *amen*!

The Body of Christ suffers with sickness and disease throughout the world and has the cure within reach. It's either collecting dust on the cocktail table or hiding in the bedroom dresser. It's easier to trust the word of the doctor because he studied medicine and knows what to prescribe for all ailments. Life is filled with surprise, and doctors practice medicine. Research is great, and I believe in finding cures for those who have no faith in the Word of God. For one to believe what medicine says over what the Creator of all things says is the greatest deception of all.

The deceitfulness of the enemy has put in minds of many, that healing went out with the last disciple and that God doesn't heal everyone. He does if you believe. "Then touched he their eyes, saying according to your faith be it unto you" (Matthew 9:29 KJV).

What do you believe? "And their eyes were opened" (Matthew 9:30 KJV). It sounds like their faith grabbed the healing. They believed Jesus was manifested in their body. The woman with the issue of blood was healed. Jesus says, "Daughter thy faith has made the whole" (Mark 5:34 KJV). "Then He said to her, "Daughter, your faith has restored you to health; go in peace and be [permanently] healed from your suffering" (Mark 5:34 AMP).

This woman had suffered with this condition for twelve years, and the doctors could not help her, but they took her money. Jesus was on the way to heal someone else's daughter, but there was a tenacious faith yearning inside this woman. Bleeding for twelve years and remaining alive was a miracle itself. Can you imagine how many pints of blood she needed a week? I tend to believe that God was refueling her bloodline. What negative talk about her did she have to endure? People then were no different than they are today. They are still doubting and operating in unbelief and holding on to and claiming the sickness rather than the healing God has provided.

She was made whole. Did God send his Word to heal? "He sent his Word, and healed them, and delivered them from their destruction" (Psalm 107:20 KJV). If we work the Word of God, by doing what God says, the power will manifest in our lives.

The Tree of life

The tree of life is just what it says. God's original plan was for humans to live forever. The tree was placed in the midst of the garden among other trees that were created. This tree's purpose was to sustain life. The tree was the most beautiful tree of all. It's polished vegetation would rejuvenate every cell in the body and restore it to its original state. The flow of fresh water from the River of Eden penetrated the deep roots and yielded life-sustaining herbs that would cause aging to cease. Imagine taking a leaf from the tree of life every day, eating it, and never having a tired bone in our bodies. Everything God creates and does is to sustain life. Adam and Eve had to be removed from the garden because of the sinful state they were in; touching the tree would have destroyed humankind forever. God's love is incomprehensible.

The tree represents the sustaining power of the God who created us all. It sustains life to those who find it and health to all their bones (Proverbs 4:22 KJV). If we adhere to the Word of God, keeping His words deeply embedded within our hearts and acting upon them, then we too are partaking of the tree of life. This tree represents purification, sanctification, authority, sovereignty, strength, wholeness, approval, and on and on. This tree could not be exhausted. The tree of life is symbolic of the Word of God in that His Word is life. It's alive, it's quick, it's sharp, and it pierces and divides.

"Who satisfies thy mouth with good things; so that thy youth is renewed like the eagle's" (Psalm 103:5 KJV). That's a bite from the tree of life. God satisfies us by extending good things to us. There are no good things that He will withhold or keep us from experiencing. The tree of life is not physically within our reach, but the scriptures are. When we immerse ourselves in what God has said and mix it with faith, we have tasted of the tree of life.

Application in principle will yield the spiritual investment of what you can believe. God breathed life into the root source to provide eternal life. Jesus shed His blood, died on the cross, and rose from the dead. His resurrection of life spiritually provided those who believe in Him access to an everlasting covenant and life. Our entire lives can be enriched with God's presence and blessings.

> According as his divine power hath given unto us all things that pertain unto life and godliness, through the knowledge of him that hath called us to glory and virtue: Whereby are given unto us exceeding great and precious promises: that ye might be partakers of the divine nature, having escaped the corruption that is in the world through lust. (2 Peter 1:3 KJV)

God has positioned us in places of spiritual power that will cause us to triumph in victory:

> For the life of the flesh is in the blood: and I have given it to you upon the altar to make an atonement for your souls: for it is the blood that makes an atonement for the soul. (Leviticus 17:11, KJV)

No longer is the blood of animals required for sacrifice. The blood of Jesus was shed once and for all for those who desire to partake of the spiritual tree of life. He has done it all, price paid in full, and we no longer have to try to work our way to God. Grab ahold to the provision that has been given you. He is the Way, the Truth, and the Life.

Surely Die?

When God gave the command not to eat or touch the tree of the knowledge of good and evil, it was for the sake of human existence. The climate and environment set forth in the Garden of Eden was supernatural, and there would never have been a need for restoration or redemption. Life was set, and every resource was provided. In the midst of Eden, two trees contained the spiritual destiny or fate that would deter the course of humanity. With all things being equal, both given the same authority and dominion to use within the earthly realm, the question of "surely die" changed the way of life for them and for generations to come.

Humans were no longer supernatural and spiritually sound; they now had to deal with the issues of life. Physical death did not occur and would have never been a factor had not the forbidden fruit been eaten. Certainly, Eve's mind began to meditate on the serpent's words: "Thou shall not surely die."

If I'm not going to surely die, then what will happen if I partake of this forbidden fruit? Will I truly be just like God? These and other questions may have entered her head. It was the ongoing conversation with the enemy and the persuasion of getting her husband, Adam, to eat that damaged their relationship with Father God.

This type of conversations remains today in the heart and mind of the believer. They wonder how close to the edge of sinful acts they can go before falling over the cliff. Among believers, there is so much sexual sin, lies, conniving, backbiting, slandering, drunkenness, and greed. God says "from such turn away" (2 Timothy 3:5 KJV).

God expects His people to be different and to be separated from what the world does in this life. "Come out from among them and be separate says the Lord of Host, and touch not the unclean thing" (2 Corinthians 6:17 KJV).

What part of "come out" do believers not understand? The church is to set the standard for the world—and not the world setting the standard for the church. Adam and Eve allowed the serpent to set a different standard for them, only realizing later that they had forfeited their original blessing.

God's righteousness must remain effective in our lives if we are to win the lost souls to Christ. We cannot say it with our mouths and live in the opposite way from what we know to be true. "Be a doer of the Word and not a hearer only" (James 1:22 KJV). Any other way is deceitful, and it is a sad day when we deceive ourselves.

If we cannot be honest with ourselves, we can't be honest with others. Listening to the lies of Satan's words cost humanity the initial relationship established in complete rulership over the entire earth, and now what we once owned has been leased out to the enemy. No, they did not die physically right away, but spiritual death occurred immediately.

Life was being in complete freedom of fellowship with the Father of creation, but then it was hidden behind fig leaves. God's intentional plan for them to live forever was shattered by one lie from the enemy, which disrupted life for all creation: thistles and thorns, sweat of the brows, sorrow, and pain. No longer did the lion lie down with the lamb. He now saw the lamb as a means of survival. God's entire creation was affected because of one disobedient act.

Thanks be to God for Jesus's completed work on the cross, which enables us to once again partake of this eternal life. Samuel told Saul "to obey is better than sacrifice" (1 Samuel 15:22 KJV). Finding ourselves in situations that can be avoided because of wrong choices, feelings of inadequacy, false perceptions of not being loved, or just doing what feels good can land us in a posture that torments the soul. The ultimate sacrifice should never trump the obedience of God's Word. There will be a cost to pay later. There are standards set by God with accountability, and we will have to answer for the deeds done on this earth.

The life assignment given before the foundation of the world was set in motion in fulfilling His plan of redemption remains a reality for the believer. Just as Eve was seeking an answer from an unauthorized, dishonest counterfeit in Eden, believers are seeking unqualified peddlers on what their assignments are. We are to inquire with the God who created us. He left you with all the answers in His Word; it's called the Bible. God really does know everything:

> "Remember the former things of old: for I am God, and there is none else; I am God, and there is none like me, declaring the end from the beginning, and from ancient times the things that are not yet done ... (Isaiah 46:9-10 KJV) God knew that man would fall, and eventually need to be redeemed, with the blueprint already set in motion, "the Lamb of God slain before the foundation of the world." (Revelation 13:8 KJV)

Jesus knew that He would become the ultimate Sacrifice for human redemption to restore our place in God. The bruising of the serpent's head is that Jesus's death and resurrection are the payment for sin.

He took on the sins of the world so that we could live again in power, in strength, in holiness, in righteousness, and in faith with His work on the cross.

Shall I surely die? This question is on the minds of those who say they believe in God, doing that which is inconsistent with the godly kind of life is a struggle of the flesh. Being led by the Spirit is the remedy for not yielding to the works of the flesh. You may not die physically right away, but spiritual death—the disconnection from God—will happen. Before long, you'll be left out of the ark of safety—alone—without help from the imposter you're listening to.

Since physical death is imminent, never allow anyone or anything to rearrange your purpose and destiny. Death will occur. "And as it is appointed unto men once to die, and after that the judgment" (Hebrews 9:27 KJV). Our prayers should be that death does not occur before we've discovered and fulfilled our purpose, reached our destiny, and left a legacy. Satan has a plan to fill our minds with seed thoughts of deception that are contrary to God's purpose for our lives. If we are deceived by our thoughts, we've tasted the forbidden fruit.

CHAPTER 4

Believe His Word

If people would genuinely take hold of the revealed truth of creation and the creative being whom God the Father, God the Son, and God the Holy Spirit sculpted during their eternal conference where specific detailed configuration and concise instructions were ascribed in the formation of humans, as spirited beings, life for most believers would be empowered.

Man and woman were formed from the dust of the earth and created in God's image and likeness, each one with power, dominion, and spiritual wisdom. The controversy of humans' creation is not questionable. Common sense explains that order is never the result of an explosion or a disaster, but if common sense is lacking, one can argue the senseless cause without rationally thinking the process through. Behind every invention, there's an inventor, behind ever design there's a designer, behind every building there's a builder, and behind creation, there is the Creator of all things: God Almighty.

Truth is revealed when we stake claim in the Spirit of truth, allowing God to abide within our spirit man. Life with God enables us to become residents of heaven as we allow Him full access to our spirits, souls, and bodies, being filled with His holy presence. Humanity was created for spiritual fellowship with Him and to acclimate Heaven's authority upon this earth. Jesus refers to himself as the Way, the Truth, and the Life—and no one can come to the Father except through Him (John 14:6 KJV). He is the Living Word.

Until we decide to seek truth in the person of Christ for ourselves, deception is inevitable. The world's view of truth is thought to be that "truth is relative." It is relative to what? How is relative truth measured? By opinions of what one believes to be truth? There is a difference between God's truth and relative truth.

God's truth never changes or proves false. It is measured through faith—something the world's standard is oblivious to—and if it can't be seen, touched, smelled, or tasted, then it's not true or real. Jesus became flesh through incarnation and entered this earthly realm to communicate the Father's will. God's truth established covenant revelation being imparted to those who will believe—that we no longer are deceived and the enemy—is defeated. God brought heaven to us. Praise God!

God assures us that he intended for His creation to reveal His presence in this earth, just as it is in heaven, being created in His image. The Bible clearly states over and over again in Genesis 1: "God said." The Word spoken manifested as sure as He said it, and the same applies to each person when the principles are applied. The very expression of His love, character, strength, righteousness, and caring heart, He has etched in the hearts of humanity to be an expression of His truth in all the earth. God and His Word are one.

"The Word of God is sharper than any two-edge sword" (Hebrews 4:12 KJV). A double-edged sword is sharpened on both sides. A sword is a bladed weapon that's intended to do great damage to a person or a thing. It slashes and thrusts much deeper than a knife. The Word of God is piercing and will divide the soul from the spirit. In any sense, the double edge will pierce and penetrate whether to correct a wrong or admonish the good. The double edge causes us to take note of our lives. The written Word of God is to be spoken with authority that will literally cause life-changing experiences and wreak havoc upon spiritual darkness.

A coworker and I became friends, and we would talk often when we worked on the same case or sat in the staff lounge. Our conversation topics included current events, basketball, occasional politics, and much conversing of the scriptures. He'd state his beliefs, and I'd share the Gospel with him. This occurred over a lengthy period of time, and I would always speak the Word of God to him and refer to where he could find a particular scripture in the Bible. Never once did I not believe that the words I spoke were piercing his trenchant wit and biting at his spirit. I knew that "faith without works is dead" (James 2:20 KJV), and I had to activate my faith and back it with the Word of God.

I purposely maintained the conversation with him because it was imperative that he came to know the truth about who Jesus is. As a very intelligent, well-read person with an empty spirit, he was hungry and searching for something to satisfy his inner cravings.

The Holy Spirit would give me the words to say, and this would arouse his curiosity. An avid debater who was willing to debate to try to prove his point, but the truth makes one free. His beliefs and thoughts were merely based upon what someone had told him about Jesus. I said, "If someone just told you about me, you would form your conclusion and reasoning based on what someone else said about me rather than giving me an opportunity to present who I am to you."

He decided to start reading the Bible, asking questions, and learning more.

I suggested that it would be wise to belong to a place of worship. That would be a viable place to learn even more. I asked if he had to attend class to earn his degree—or if it happened at home without attending classes or reading the required materials and textbooks. This took place before there were online classes.

He said, "Yes, I guess I did."

I explained that in the same way knowledge was needed for his education, the same effort should be applied to learn who Jesus is. The end result was that he found a church and converted to the faith by surrendering his life to the Lord.

After some weeks, he shared some good news with me. He had accepted the Lord into his heart, and his life had changed. "It was during a visit to church with a friend that I gave my life to God."

"Lord, Jesus," I exclaimed. I was so thrilled that all I could do was thank and praise God right where I stood. The Word works. This is only the beginning of an excited life in Christ because I continued to pour into his soul.

God's Word marinates the spirit. Living a godly life can change a life and wreak havoc in the enemy's camp.

I continued to feed my coworker the Word of God and explained that God's Spirit needed to remain faithful in him to this new empowering life in Christ. That was to be filled with the gift of the Holy Spirit. I spent every opportunity sharing scriptures that referred to being filled with the Holy Spirit. Before long, God ministered to him, and he was filled with more of God's presence. I continued encouraging him to spend as much time as possible in prayer and asking God for the infilling of His presence.

"And they were all filled with the Holy Ghost, and began to speak with other tongues, as the Spirit gave them utterance" (Acts 2:4 KJV).

Apostle Paul asked a certain group of people "Have you received the Holy Ghost since ye believed?" (Acts 19:2 KJV). A short time later, he came and spoke about having the experience with God filling him with His presence. "I was at home praying and asking God to fill me with the Holy Spirit, and all of a sudden I began speaking in tongues and couldn't stop." This experience in God's presence increased his faith. He now knows that what was spoken was the truth. The Word of God speaks to every situation, circumstance, encounter, and season. We speak the Word, we believe, and we receive.

God's Word is just as sure as the neck is connected to your head. When we speak the Word out of our mouths, its faith creates a tangible substance. Mixing faith with scripture and believing when you pray the Word works for healing, finances, family issues, and anything else:

> If you abide in me, and my words abide in you, ye shall ask what ye will, and it shall be done unto you. Herein is my Father glorified, that ye bear much fruit; so, shall ye be my disciples. (John 15:7–8 KJV)

It's simply working the Word of God, because His "shall" is loaded. I once heard someone say, "That we don't have any trouble—all we need is to have faith in God." Believe His Word!

CHAPTER 5

Watch Out—It's Alive

> Through faith we understand that the worlds were
> framed by the Word of God, so that things which are
> seen were not made of things which do appear.
> —Hebrews 11:3 (KJV)

Our finite minds are limited in deciphering the magnitude of how God spoke a word that created what He said. It's through revelation that we gain understanding in believing what God says is true. It is by faith that our spiritual life is activated to receive what heaven declares to be so. Everything He spoke into existence in Genesis remains and continues to be since the beginning of time. Everything produces after its kind; God said, "The seed is in itself" (Genesis 1:11 KJV).

The seed-bearing fruit and vegetation could only be reproduced by life in the spoken word that spawn life to the seed. Jesus is the absolute reason His Word is alive. He is the "Living Word. He is the Way, the Truth, and the Life (John 14:6 KJV). Allow the seed to germinate within you.

Faith in God gives life to the words you speak long as its scripturally based. Words are powerful, and when you have God backing your words, the force of strength is potent enough to demolish your mountain. God's Word is attached with principle, which causes an overwhelming strategic disabling in the enemy's camp. Faith generates compelling action in the Spirit that parts the heavens and gains the attention of the Father who alerts the Holy Spirit to release the blessing to the angelic beings assigned to you, bearing conclusive evidence. Believe you received it when you pray. Praying is speaking the Word of God when we pray according to scripture. One of my favorite scriptures is: "Therefore I say unto you, what things so ever you desire, when you pray, believe that you received them, and you shall have them" (Mark 11:24 KJV). As I stated in an earlier chapter, "God's *shall* is loaded."

I remember my first time seeing a Mercedes-Benz. As a little girl, I found it fascinating. With an honest heart, I said to God, "I want to own that type of automobile one day." That is pretty much it. I remember seeing people in the car with the windows rolled up. I thought, *Why are the windows rolled up? It is so hot today.* We didn't have air-conditioning in our car, and I had no idea why the windows were rolled up. Something about that vehicle settled my heart, and I knew that one day God was going to give me one. I never stopped believing.

While I was employed at an institution with an hourly rate of $5.45, the mere thought of ever owning that Mercedes was debatable. At that rate of pay, I could never see my dream fulfilled. I remembered what I said to God and decided to work on increasing my faith to cause this thing to become the evidence of what was definitely not there. Several years passed, and with time, my faith increased because I heard the Word of God intentionally. I scheduled appointments with Him to feed my faith. "Faith comes by hearing the Word" (Romans 10:17 KJV). I listened faithfully and studied scripture because I had the promise of my heavenly Father God in my heart. You must see him as Father.

"No good thing would He withhold from them that walk uprightly" (Psalm 84:11 KJV), which includes me. I knew the way to get results to my prayers was to simply work God's Word. If you "believe when you pray, you shall have it" (Mark 11:24 KJV). That included me.

If His Word abides in you, and you abide in His Word, you can ask what you will—and it will be done unto you (John 15:7 KJV). That included me. I was blessed with a brand-new Mercedes Benz in the middle of my first year of Bible School. The three things I purposed to learn there were how to pray, how to walk by faith, and how to know the voice of God. I kept believing that when I spoke the Word of God, the life in His Word penetrated the faith realm and manifested in the physical realm! His Word is life to anyone who is willing to seek it out, find it, believe it, and speak it.

John, the beloved disciple of Jesus, had supernatural vision as to who Jesus was. His Gospel account differs from that of the other disciples. John's spiritual antenna beamed high into the heavens, and revelations were downloaded. That would be a written guide for those who desired to seek deeper insights and wisdom as to who the Son of Man is rather than gleaning superficially and never understanding the Sanctifier of our souls.

John is often referred to as "The Revelator." John wrote of Jesus being the "Bread of life, the Lamb of God, the Light of the world, the Resurrection and the Life, the Son of Man, the Son of God, and an intercessor." He knew revelation and spiritual discernment:

> In the beginning was the Word, and the Word was with God, and the Word was God. The same was in the beginning with God. (John 1:1–2 KJV)

John's penning refers to the original conformation of how it all began. He refers to the Living Word of God: Jesus. He reveals the true essence of who Christ is, what He came to do, and how He is the substance for whatever is needed. It is in Him. What is written was spoken before it ever came to be.

It's On—and It's Popping

The Word of God says, "It's the Spirit that quickens; and the flesh profits nothing: the words that I speak unto you they are spirit, and they are life" (John 6:63 KJV). The Word of God invigorates our inner being and launches our spiritual receptors to come alive. Supernatural encounters enable believers to extract power from the Word of God, which places them in positions of authority.

God's Word is better than money in the bank. There is a massive amount of people with millions in their bank accounts around the world, and not one of those dollars can heal their disease. Having financial substance is a good thing in this natural realm, but without the Word of God to penetrate the supernatural realm when it's needed, they remain hanging in the wing. God's Word can heal the sickly, unleash strongholds, and give sight to physical and spiritual blindness.

The Word is attributed to seeds, and the planting of the seeded Word of God creates and manifests simply by watering the Word with faith. Faith is just taking the Father at His Word and knowing that what you believe is what you will receive. If you believe something in the negative realm, it will manifest. We sometimes wonder why certain things happen in life, but it's because we had more faith in it than focus in on what's true: God's Word. His Word was sent to heal (Psalm 107:20 KJV).

I'm reminded of the woman with the issue of blood who spent all her money seeing doctors and didn't receive healing until she heard about Jesus coming to town. The word came to her that the Healer was in the streets of Galilee. Her spiritual receptors sparked through faith, and she knew if she could get close enough to Jesus to touch the hem of His garment, His power would be extracted through her faith. He would do what the doctors could not do.

The anointed power to heal was upon Jesus, and it was up to her to believe, release her faith, and withdraw from the Source. The Living Word of God was present then as He is today. It is according to your faith that grants approval of what you believe in. Jesus said, "Daughter, your faith has made thee whole" (Mark 5:34 KJV).

While on assignment, I gathered pertinent information that would assist me in doing my job. I noticed a heartbreaking diagnosis in a young person. Righteous indignation came upon me in that room. I experienced a strong sense of anger about how the enemy had attacked the young person. I said to God, "No, the devil has to take his hand off of them. They are too young and have a lot of life before them." I served the enemy notice and said, "Today, Devil, you will take your filthy hands off of them." I had not seen the patient yet, but I knew what I knew. I knew the Word of God was on my side, that I would speak to that disease, and that it would depart their body.

I approached the pre op area and I reviewed the chart to ensure that nothing was missing on the computer. I glanced over to the spot where they were stationed and said to God, "This is a beautiful-looking person, and that the devil's work has to be destroyed."

God cleared the way for His work to be performed.

I chose to go speak to the patient as the pre op nurse was leaving, and I do not remember seeing them anymore. I went over to assess the patient, asked all my questions, and offered to let them ask questions of me.

I said, "I feel led to pray for you because God wants to heal your body."

Their response was affirmative.

As I pulled the curtain, I asked the patient if the person with them was their parent, and it was. I looked straight in the parent's eye and asked if they minded us praying.

They said, "Please do."

I said, "I need you to stay in faith with me—and you cannot doubt. Not even for a second, no doubting. Can you believe with me?" I spoke firmly and faithfully because I knew God's anointing to heal was present. I felt Him.

They said "Yes, I will believe and not doubt."

I said "Can you stay in faith to believe for your healing."

The patient responded, "Yes."

I began to pray, and I knew that God was doing what he directed me to do when I prayed with them. The Holy Spirit's presence touched both so powerfully. I prayed until I had a release from God, and then I spoke these words with divine authority: "I will take you back here, but when the doctor opens you up, he will find no tumor in your body."

I wheeled them into the operating room and asked what side of their body the cancer was on.

They said, "On the right side."

I asked if they minded if I laid hands on that part of their body and prayed for that as well. I did, believing what I knew to be true: God's Word.

In the operating room, I assisted them to the table, positioned them, and secured them.

After the general anesthetic was administered, the patient was prepped for surgery.

The case was boarded for a couple of hours. After the second timeout, the doctor began with making the incision and looking inside the patient. After fifteen to twenty minutes of exploration, they could not find a tumor. The doctor said, "We are done. There is no tumor in here."

I immediately said, "Did you hear the doctor?"

The nurse said, "No, I didn't hear him."

I said, "He said there is no tumor in the body." I wanted to take a giant leap into the heavens and hug God's neck. I had never met this person, and I knew nothing about them except that God wanted them healed from this sickening disease that the enemy had put on them.

We finished the case and transported them to the recovery room. I hurried back to my room to clean out the extra supplies and equipment, I went as fast as I could to find the patient's family. They stood down the hall with smiles on their faces that were larger than life. I asked if the doctor had spoken with them, but their facial expressions said it all. We rejoiced and praised God together. I said, "Stay in faith."

The Word of God is already established and settled in heaven, and it's up to us to take what's been spoken and written to heart, believe it, and watch it work on our behalf. No matter what comes against you, who tries to destroy you, or what sickness the enemy dares to put upon you, the Word of God is alive and is the cure for whatever ails you. His Word is always right—and the results are on and popping.

It's Lit: Put the Spotlight on It

I was led to attend Bible school by the prompting of the Spirit of God. I arrived there in the piping hot summer with the purpose of learning three spiritual disciplines: how to pray, how to recognize the voice of God, and how to live by faith and walk out His promises. I set out making a covenant with God that I would do everything humanly possible in commitment with Him to accomplish this goal. The flame burning on the inside to know more was to my imagination what it was like for Jeremiah when he expressed that God's Word is "like fire shut up in his bones" (Jeremiah 20:9 KJV).

Fire is bright, it gives light, it radiates heat, it can be a blessing or a curse, and it is hot. You just cannot sit on fire! Fire creates an excitement phase whether you are at a bonfire or watching a building burn down. There was a fiery passion with an intense devotion to hear from God, which led my desire, knowing it would only increase. The hunger and thirst grew rapidly as time passed.

Before I was moved to go to Bible school, God spoke to me from the book of Isaiah. I found myself reading these chapters every day for weeks:

> Enlarge the place of thy tent, and let them stretch forth the curtains of thy habitations, spare not, lengthen thy cords, and strengthen thy stakes. (Isaiah 54:2 KJV)

> For thy Maker is thine husband; the Lord of host is his name; and thy Redeemer the Holy One of Israel; The God of the whole earth shall he be called. For the Lord hath called thee as a woman forsaken and grieved in spirit, and a wife of youth, when thou were refused, says thy God. (Isaiah 54:5–6 KJV)

This was fresh and alive to me. I'd been forsaken by the one who was supposed to love me till death did us part. Faithful and committed, I was loving the Lord with all I had inside me. I was raising my son in the admonition of the Lord, teaching him to love God, and living godly before him in our home.

One day, my husband came home and said, "I don't think I want to be married anymore."

Was I hurt by those words? Yes. Did I allow the flesh to manifest? No. I softly responded, "Okay, if that's what you want. But if you get out there and find that is not what you want, the door will be open." I realized the words spoken from my mouth were from a different domain of influence. It was as if God had reached down, covered my mouth, and replied.

It was beyond the carnal realm of what I was experiencing; it was truly supernatural. Rejection is not comfortable, and it radiates negative vibes, which tends to place you in a different zone. I found myself speaking kind words as if I felt no pain or hurt from what was said by the man I had planned to spend the rest of my life with. The Living Word of God illuminated my spirit, which created a soothing atmosphere that could have easily been disastrous with words of strife in retaliation. The Holy Spirit spoke through me with a soft answer that stimulated the love of God being portrayed in me. I knew that his spirit remained unregenerate.

Yes, every emotion known to a hurting woman was experienced, and it was a fight of faith to remain strong and committed to what God had said. God said, "For thy Maker is thy Husband" (Isaiah 54:5 KJV). As I searched the scriptures to find peace in my soul, joy for my heart, and to continue having a desire for the one I was in covenant with, I mobilized every spiritual discipline I knew to defeat the enemy. Prayer is such a powerful discipline, and it organizes the strategic plan of God.

We should invite Him to handle our issues, to give understanding in the devised plan, and to follow through when we feel helpless or disconnected. His plans are always the opposite of what the carnal mind and human nature will think or do. I began to pray for him since the Bible tells us to "pray for them which despitefully use you" (Luke 6:28 KJV). Being kind and graceful helps defeat the works of the enemy. As I fought every emotion to slay the flesh and keep it in check, I saw God beginning to work. He was back home in two weeks.

I had to continue praying and allow my spirit to take charge of the carnal self in order not to operate foolishly. The mind thinks along the sensuous route, which makes a place for the enemy to damage the heart and try to hurt him somehow. It pays to do it God's way. One profound thing I learned was that your plans may pay you now, but they will cost you later. God's plans may cost you now, but they will pay you later.

Naaman thought it was foolish to obey what Elisha spoke concerning his healing. He was a man of valor, a captain of host to Syria's king, and a man of stature: "But he was a leper" (2 Kings 5:1 KJV). He was in need of supernatural healing for his body with a spirit of disobedience among his members. He needed an intervention of heaven's grace. His initial plan was not to adhere to the word given, and he wondered why two other rivers were not chosen for him to dip in.

Frustrated with the king of Israel, he tore his clothes once he read the letter prior to hearing from Elisha. He refused to come out to speak with him, but he sent word by a messenger. Can you imagine what crossed his mind? *Do they know who I am? Who does this prophet think he is, not allowing me in to speak with him? I have a close relationship with the King of Syria.*

Nothing has changed. There are still people who say they love God with this same attitude in the church Jesus built, but we know they operate from the spirit within.

We can speculate on and on about what Naaman was feeling. The Bible says he was "wroth and went away in a rage" (2 Kings 5:11, 12 KJV) from Elisha's house. What Naaman failed to understand was that the Word is alive. The word spoken by Elisha was as if Naaman heard it from the mouth of God. In the Old Testament, God spoke through prophets to speak to the people.

The word came to Naaman three times: once through the young maiden who served his wife, secondly through the prophet Elisha, and then through his servants who helped him see from a different perspective.

> If the prophet had bid thee do some great thing, would you not have done it? How much rather then, when he says to thee Wash and be clean? (2 Kings 5:13 KJV)

Naaman's spirit was quickened, and the Word came alive in him. Thank God for surrounding us with people who are a little wiser than we are. The end of this story is God's Word working as He originally designed it to be.

Once Naaman's noncompliant spirit was defeated, the glorious light shined, he obeyed, and healing manifested:

> So shall my word be that goes forth out of my mouth: it shall not return unto me void, but it shall accomplish that which I please, and it shall prosper in the thing whereto I sent it. (Isaiah 55:11 KJV)

The Spirit of God moved upon man in the Old Testament, and He spoke through the mouth of the prophets. In the New Covenant, God moves on the inside of man. There is a light on the inside. It's lit, and all we're required to do is let it shine through. Jesus said, "I am the Light of the world" (John 8:12 KJV).

Believers struggle with the prophetic voice and miss the plan of God. God gave five gifts that to the church. "And He gave some, apostles; and some, prophets; and some, evangelists; and some, pastors and teachers" (Ephesians 4:11 KJV).

There is purpose in the use of these gifts. God expects his church to be perfected so the work of the ministry can be carried out and lives can be changed. He wants His body to be built up, robust, and spiritually sound. It's His desire that all human beings come full circle into the unity of the knowledge of Jesus and be made perfect in the fullness of the stature of Christ (Ephesians 4:12–13 KJV). I have yet to see a church where all five gifts are present and in operation.

Most churches have a pastor and associate ministers on staff. The Bible is preached, praise and worship happen, ushers and greeters welcome you at the door to seat you, and obscure smiles are deceiving. The hurt and pain of believers are camouflaged behind the clothes and makeup we wear, our economic status, the cars we drive, the positions we hold, and the art of masking. It is not the church that Jesus established.

The massive gatherings were held in fields, and He made house calls. We can read about people being delivered, being set free from oppression, receiving forgiveness, being healed, feeding from a small lunch, two fish, and a loaf of bread, being raised from the dead, blind eyes opening, the lame walking, the deaf hearing, and demonic spirits being cast out into the sea. Miracles!

The work of the church was carried out after the ascension of Jesus. The apostles were filled with the Holy Spirit and spoke God's Word. The very one who denied Jesus after being filled with the Spirit of God preached, and thousands of souls were transformed to righteousness. Peter's bait was the Word of God. Luke wrote an account to Theophilus:

> All the things Jesus began to do and to teach until the day when He ascended to heaven, after He had by the Holy Spirit given instruction to the apostle to those whom he had chosen. (Acts 1:1–2 AMP)

During the forty days after Jesus's resurrection, he spoke to the apostles and referred to the kingdom of God and God's way of doing things. He taught royal power, dominion, and ruling with the authority of heaven, which is given to every believer to operate in. With instructions for the upper-room experience, every believer has the opportunity to reside there until the fulfillment of the promise. God always has a remnant. The 120 souls who were diligent in seeking after what was spoken by Jesus were steadfast in their faith, and in that room, they received the infilling of God's presence. They were given a heavenly language that would change who they were and their lives forever.

The awesome power of heaven, now abiding inside men and women, is accessible today. We can do what the apostles did on an even greater level.

> Verily, verily, I say unto you, He that believeth on me, the works that I do shall he do also; and Greater works than these shall ye do because I go unto my Father. (John 14:12 KJV)

As Peter and John walked into the temple, a lame man was asking for alms. Peter, being full of faith, said, "Look on us." Peter had inside information about what this man needed and saw beyond what would meet his need at that moment:

> Silver and gold have I none; but such as I have, I give unto you: In the name of Jesus Christ of Nazareth, rise up and walk. (Acts 3:6 KJV)

Peter acted on what he believed, took the lame man by the right hand, and lifted him up:

"suddenly his feet and ankle bones received strength" (Acts 3:7 KJV). Every cell in the man's ankles came alive. He received the strength to walk, and there was a revelation deposited in his spirit when Peter spoke: "He leaped to praise God" (Acts 3:8 KJV). I can imagine that the feeling in his inner being caused him to move with resounding haste.

Connecting with the words Peter spoke, this man's reality was no longer hindered by what held him captive. The encounter placed a surge in his soul and a spring in his step. God's Word operated as God determined it to do so. The Word is alive; it just needs to be spoken in faith and believed.

The revelation of God's power once illuminated in our spirit will cause the supernatural to be understood. During a Sunday morning prayer time, a woman said, "I need God to heal the cancer in my breast." The Lord spoke to me as she was sharing her story. I was asked by one of the leaders to pray for her. I said, "God already spoke to me to lay hands on her, and He will heal her." I did what God instructed me to do.

I laid my hand on her body and prayed. The fire of the Holy Spirit began to eradicate the cancer and I felt a warmness in my left hand. I said, "When you see the doctor in Chicago, they will not find a lump in your breast because God just healed you." She had to take a trip to Chicago to see the specialist the following Tuesday. On the day of her appointment, I received a text from her:

> Just wanted to tell you thanks for all your prayers and laying on of hands. They know they could not find anything—I mean nothing. They could not understand because they felt it, but nothing showed up when they shot the radiation dye in. So, thank God for Jesus and thanks to all who stood in the gap for me. Thanks, mighty anointed woman of God.

She spoke to me at church the following Sunday and said, "When you laid your hand on me, it was so hot. It was like fire."

I said, "Yes, it is like fire—the fire of the Holy Spirit."

I remembered Jeremiah's words: "It's like fire shut up in my bones."

She told me how they just stood there and scratched their heads because they couldn't figure it out. God's Word will always trump science. His Word always ranks above your situation and circumstance when you believe that which you speak. The Word of God was prayed over her. They were not my words; it was scripture's prayers.

When the scriptures are prayed, the power of God is released. His words are being spoken just as they were in the beginning. When

God spoke, it came to be. When a believer speaks the Word of God, God has to do what you say it's His Word. His Word is as real as the foot attached to your ankle. There is an application to the manifesting of what you speak. His Word must be mixed with faith without any shadow of doubt.

Love is the main ingredient in the mix because "faith works by love" (Galatians 5:6 KJV). God is love; that is who He is. He expects His creation to operate in that love. This is what a lot of believers miss. It is in the love walk; oh, it's easy to love those who love us. The challenge is loving those who do not love you and those who mistreat you or say negative things about you when you've done nothing to harm them. Some people will just not like the way you appear to them without even having a relationship or a conversation with you.

> Love your enemies; Bless those who curse you, do good to them that hate you, pray for those who despitefully use you. (Matthew 5:44 KJV)

I often say to people, especially believers, "You must learn to work God's Word." That means speaking the Word over every condition and place you find yourself in life. It is the power behind what we believe. It is the game changer. God will work on you and the person involved. Do not think for a minute that you can't use a spiritual adjustment.

God wants to acclimate us to the spiritual realm of where we are to live. The mistreatment from someone else will cause an alteration in your spirit, and God wants you delivered as well. We have to learn that it's not the person standing before us; it's a contrary spirit that's been given a place to operate in them. When we walk out Matthew 5:44, God has to intervene and change the heart. The next time you encounter that person, it will be in a new light—and you will no longer see them after the flesh.

Change occurs in you, and you see them the way God does. The love of God will manifest. I know what I am talking about. The Word works, and it is lit. All we're required to do is shine the light. Jesus is the light of the world. Applied principle yields great results.

I share these real-life stories to help increase your faith and to let you see that the Word of God remains alive. During my time at

Bible school, it was made aware to me that there was a man who had interest in me while another lady had interest in him. When I occasionally had a conversation with him, she would show up and want to take over the conversation. I would politely excuse myself and go to my next class. I would make sure that I carried lotion and tissue paper in my purse in case someone had a need and I could be a blessing. When she needed lotion or a tissue, I would offer them to her, and she thanked me. I would speak to her every time I saw her, and I continued to show her the love of God.

One day, as I was talking to another student in the hall, she deliberately knocked my books out of my hand and said, "Oh I'm sorry. Excuse me."

I smiled, told her it was okay, and picked up my belongings.

I believe this happened because the guy would purposely seek me out in between classes and walk me to class, and she did not appreciate it. I never said a negative word to her concerning the incident. Several students knew how she felt about him and how he felt about me, and they didn't mind voicing their opinions. He was a wonderful man who loved God and lived godly—no matter where you saw him. He was such a balanced man that I literally gave him the name "Mr. Wonderful."

I lived Matthew 5:44 because I wanted to be the child of my Father in heaven. She stopped her personal harassment and started being nice to me when she realized I would not step outside of what I believed: the Word of God. She was transformed—and so was I. My faith increased, and God led me onto greater works.

God's work for us is to believe in Jesus, heaven coming down to us, and the One sent by the Father to show us the way. The kingdom of God is here. Just tap into it to see the mighty works of the Holy Spirit done through the willingness of you, the believer. "These signs shall follow them that believe" (Mark 16:17 KJV). It's lit—now shine the light on it!

Is the fire of God lit in your world? Are you operating according to the Word of truth? Are you in the way of what God's trying to do in your life? Just seed the thoughts and meditate on them.

Faithful participation in the ways of God will cause an eruption in the spirit for your world with an unlimited presence of His power to be turned upside down. Paul and Silas ripped up the enemy's camp. The nonbelievers in the book of Acts heard the Word of God and experienced the Word of God:

> The Word was made flesh and dwelt among us. (John 1:14 KJV)

> God said, let us make man. (Genesis 1:26 KJV)

To whom was he speaking? The fullness of the Trinity—the Father, the Son, and the Holy Spirit—was present during the strategic summit of human creation. Life as we know it came into existence because of the words spoken by the Creator of all things.

As sons and daughters representing our heavenly Father in this earthly realm—through the Lordship of His Son, Jesus Christ—we've been given permission to use His name and receive the same benefit as the Son based on His Father's word. He has empowered and granted us to operate in His authority. Watch out—the Word is alive!

CHAPTER 6

Sharpen Your Sword

My Slash-Proof Suit

God provided armor for the entire army of believers with the intention of it never being defeated. The scripture clearly says to "put on the whole armor of God" (Ephesians 6:11 KJV). That allows us to take part in the plan of God. He made provisions for the battles of life and equipped the saints to withstand the enemy on all grounds. He will always cause us to triumph.

If you are caught off guard and life is bottoming out, it's time to put on your armor. That instruction is clear. It is like to dressing up for an evening out. We are suited up and ready to step out in public with our hair combed, polished apparel, and flip-flops. This armor must be worn in its entirety. We are to be suited in the whole armor of God in order to be covered on all sides.

The purpose of the armor is to stand against whatever the devil sends your way—deceit, imposters, sickness, and disease—to destroy your life. A wicked spirit lurks around us. It wants to terrorize and abort the plan God mapped out for our lives. The coverage God gives will protect the vital areas of our lives.

Our loins are surrounded with *truth*. The reproductive organs are housed in the pelvic area. We were commissioned "to be fruitful and multiply" (Genesis 1:26 KJV). The *breastplate of righteousness* protects our hearts, lungs, and diaphragms. We are to have hearts after God and live in his righteousness. When our hearts are right, our lives are cheerful.

Our feet are preserved with the preparation of the *gospel of peace*. We are supposed to allow God's peace to rule in our hearts. His promise to keep us in perfect peace is sure when our minds remain on Him. The *shield of faith* will extinguish every fiery thing the attacker sends against us. The shield will protect us and intercept from close range or from afar. God is our protector, and He will shield us (Ephesians 6: 14–16 KJV).

It matters not if weare being attacked; the shield blocks and protects from the weaponry of the enemy. The *helmet of salvation* provides protection for our brains, which regulate our thought patterns, and the mind. We are to have "the mind of Christ" (1 Corinthians 2:12 KJV). If satanic lies enter our heads, and we dwell upon them for long enough, we start to believe them. If we act upon them because they have entered our hearts, we will have distorted thinking. That is truly not the thought of God.

God has given the believer an outer spiritual protective defense, five pieces of armor, and one weapon. "The *Sword of the Spirit*, which is the Word of God" (Ephesians 6:13–17, NKJV). The Word of God cuts asunder and divides the soul from the spirit. God likens His Word to a sword.

In one scripture, God's Word is "sharper than a two-edged sword" (Hebrews 4:12 KJV). How powerful can a person be with a sword in their hand when they have perfected themselves and mastered the art of its use.

A sword is made to be a slashing and battering weapon that's aimed to knock down an opponent and defeat them. There is no chance of them being a threat anymore. The sword is great in length, and you need not get right up on the opponent to cause injury. God's Word is to be spoken to defeat our problems, our lingering situations, and our persistent happenstance. Use the Word of God to slash the issue with scripture that you know is true.

Destroy the works of the enemy in your life by speaking God's Word with authority. Get a revelation of knowing that the "Son of God was manifested that He might destroy the works of the devil" (1 John 3:8 KJV). Jesus awarded us His name to use and the written Word to know. What is your excuse? Why are you defeated? Why are you not walking in victory since your heavenly Father has nothing but good news for us?

Have you ever noticed that He didn't give us anything to protect our backs? Why? God never intended for a believer to run from the enemy. We are to stand face to face, flatfooted, and grounded with a tenacious faith and God's Word fixed and established in our spirits.

I speak with certainty that the Word of God is already settled and irrefutable. That which I speak shall be performed. God told Jeremiah what He planned before Jeremiah was in his mother's womb: "For you shall go to all to whom I send you, and whatever I command you, you shall speak" (Jeremiah 1:7 NKJV). God's vision of Jeremiah was quite different from Jeremiah's vision of himself.

God has a master plan for every individual. It is supernatural, in plain view of the Spirit, and obscured to the natural fleshly sense: "Ah no Lord, I do not know how to speak, for I am only a young man" (Jeremiah 1:6–7 AMP).

God had to sound the alarm and shake things up. Jeremiah disconnected from the natural and connected to the supernatural stimulation of what he was purposed to do. God was backing him as his rear guard and assuring him that he need not fear anything.

> "Do not be afraid of them [or their hostile faces], For I am with you [always] to protect you and deliver you," says the Lord. Then the Lord stretched out His hand and touched my mouth, and the Lord said to me, "Behold (hear Me), I have put My words in your mouth. See, I have appointed you this day over the nations and the kingdoms, to uproot and break down, to destroy and to overthrow, to build and to plant." (Jeremiah 1:8–10 AMP)

> For I am [actively] watching over my word to fulfill it. (Jeremiah 1:12 AMP)

God was saying, "If you say what I've instructed you to say, I'll do what you say." He will always watch over His Word and perform it.

Fear is a dreadful spirit that attacks and hinders us from carrying out the call of God. When altar calls are made for salvation, people fight against coming because of fear. The Spirit of God tells you to speak a word to that sister, but you fear rejection. God tells you to leave this job and move somewhere else, but you experience the fear of the unknown. Fear is a spirit, and it is what we do with the arrest that determines the end result. Fear must be counteracted with faith.

When fear attacks your spirit, just release love from your inner being:

> God did not give us the spirit of fear, but of power, love, and a sound mind. (2 Timothy 1:7 KJV)
>
> Perfect love cast out all fear. (1 John 4:18 KJV)

God's antidote nullifies the satanic poison of fear and false evidence appearing real. Fear is described as "a distressing emotion aroused by impending danger, evil, pain, or something that's not yet understood, whether the threat is real or imagined; the feeling or condition of being afraid" (Dictionary.com). It is not the reverential awe referred to as the "fear of God."

There is no fear in love. God's love is perfect, it is without restraint, and it's what held Jesus on the cross. It gives strength and enhances trust. His love enables freedom to be who He created you to become. His love will change our hearts from stony to hearts of flesh when we allow Him to pour out into us.

When I was a teenager, the girls in our class began to experience emotions for the opposite sex. They would share their feelings among one another but were afraid to tell the person they were interested in. I asked, "Why not let them know?" Most of the time, they said, "I'm too scared." That fear held them back from going after what they desired. It was not until the other person was made aware that a relationship could be established.

Once their feelings were known and the two became friends—spending time talking and getting to know one another—their love evolved and cast out the fear. They were no longer slaves to the spirit of fear because their feelings had been expressed and received. Love prevailed, and anxiety was eradicated.

There are times when we want to come to the Lord, but because we are bound in spiritual darkness, fear grips our hearts. It releases panic in giving God our all because we have not been taught about His perfect love. We think there is no way He can love us because we have chosen to live without acknowledging Him. They think they have committed an unpardonable sin—and there is no way God could ever forgive them. They think they will someday fix things to satisfy God and reunite with Him.

I've witnessed to so many people, including family members, who have said, "I will when I get myself together." If we could get ourselves together, Jesus would not have left heaven to die for the redemption of humankind. When we receive His love and experience His grace, fear is cast out. God's perfect love through us drives out fear. God's perfect love is a *weapon* for fear. He never gave us "the spirit of fear," but He gave us "love, power, and a sound mind." (2 Timothy 1:7 KJV). Praises to the Lord! Let's use what He gave us! The more you use the Word of God, the sharper your sword will be.

In the Trenches

A spiritual military, the army of the Lord, has frontline warriors to seek the face of God through prayer, fasting, worship, and meditation of the Word. They wreck the enemy's camp. They are the ones you will find in the trenches—suited and ready for battle. Military gear is not for lightweights. Seventy to eighty pounds are added to the fatigues that are necessary for survival in addition to the weapon that must be carried. "The weapons of our warfare are not carnal, but mighty through God to the pulling down of strongholds" (2 Corinthians 10:4 KJV).

The sword of the Spirit, which is the mouth of God, shall defuse the attacker. Praying the scriptures is a powerful weapon that I use all the time. I know God will be doing just what he said he'd do.

The sword sharpened on both sides readily destroys the works of the enemy. Spending time in the Word of God and making deposits for your spirit is like eating food to nourish the body. Believers have no problem feeding their bodies several meals a day that might not be wholesome, and they struggle to feed their spirits one Snack Pack lunch per week.

Job said, "Neither have I gone back from the commandment of his lips; I have esteemed the words of his mouth more than my necessary food" (Job 23:12 KJV). It's imperative that we feed our spirit man daily.

A sharpened sword will slash the opponent into pieces. Meditation on God's Word is the basis for a battle-ready sword. Careful attention is to be maintained when you're sharpening a sword. You must be engaged 100 percent while performing this task. You cannot become diverted with outside interference and not expect to cause harm to yourself. Focusing on the work at hand will influence the outcome of your victory.

The diligence in studying God's Word sharpens you with an advantage to supernaturally destroy the devil's camp. The grace of God enables one to maintain the ability to pull down the strongholds.

In the 1990s, after working twelve hours at the hospital, I went to the evening service of worship. It was Resurrection Sunday, and the theatrics of the Easter story were being portrayed. I planned to meet up with a sister from church who had taken my two sons to the service. By the time I arrived, the program had already begun. The sanctuary was dark, and I was seated by an usher. I wrapped myself up in the amazing performance of ordinary people in church. I thought, *Hollywood has nothing on this*. The props, the live animals, the costume design, the lighting, the sound, and the story line portrayed was scripturally accurate.

I will never forget one scene because it changed my life forever. During the scene when Jesus went to Lazarus's grave to raise him up, the man who played Jesus turned to the woman in the role of Martha and said, "Said I not unto thee, that, if thou would believe, thou should see the glory of God?" (John 11:40 KJV). The word *believe* came alive for me. My spirit was quickened.

Suddenly, I began to weep nonstop, knowing the revelation of God's Word had just been deposited into my spirit. I said to God, "It's simply believing your Word." I felt His presence all over me. It was like fresh oil being poured from the heavens with revelation in a whole new light. From that day on, I was determined to be and do what I learned of the revealed truth of Jesus's Word: believe.

There were such a massive crowd that I was not able to find my dear sister who had my children. I decided to leave and pick them up from her home. As I walked to the car and drove, the tears came. I couldn't stop praising and thanking God for the revelation I had just received.

When I arrived home, the boys welcomed me and said, "Momma, did someone mess with you? What's wrong?"

I said, "No one has bothered me. I've just been with God, and I don't think He is finished with me. I need to go into my room alone with God so He can complete what He's doing in me." My bedroom was my prayer room, and I thanked God, praised God, and felt His powerful presence there. It was the beginning of the healing anointing that I was to operate in under his direction and timing.

In 1993, I was in my second year of Bible school. I went home that summer to visit my mother. I was there for one week, and the day before I was supposed to leave, I realized that I had not contacted one of my sister friends. If she knew I was in town and did not get in touch with her, I would not hear the end of it.

I decided to go to her job and see her there. When I arrived, the Holy Spirit said, "Go home." I clearly heard Him say it. I immediately turned the car around and headed back to my mother's house. Michael, my youngest son, was around six. He said, "Momma, I thought we were going to see Breocha."

I said, "Yes, we were, but God said to go home—and that's where we are going."

I arrived home in about five minutes and went in the house with no idea why God had redirected my plans. I simply obeyed and did as I heard in the Spirit. Ten minutes later, my niece came over with her baby in her arms. The last time I saw her, she had been pregnant. I said, "How old is he?"

She said that he was seven months old, but he was underweight and slow in developing because he was born with a hole in his heart and Down syndrome.

Before I knew it, I had taken him into my arms. I began to walk and pray God's Word over this baby. I prayed with fervency and in faith, believing every word I spoke.

I will never forget the look on her face as I walked through the living room with her child and declared the Word to be so. After God gave me release, I stopped praying and said, "I do not care what the doctors say or what report was given, God has healed your baby today." I instructed her to meditate on every healing scripture in the Word of God, speak His Word over this child, and *believe* God. I knew without a doubt that the work was finished and why God had interrupted my day: to get His plan done on behalf of this little child. I touched base with Breocha and flew back to Tulsa the next day.

Months went by with no word from my niece about the baby. I would say to God, "Why won't she call me and say something? If she does not, I know You healed him." God led me to remain in Broken Arrow for another year after graduation. Tulsa had a presence of God that I never wanted to leave. I waited to leave until I heard from Him.

I was praying at the Bible school when I heard a voice say, "Your time here is finished." I immediately turned around, but there was no one behind me. I said, "Okay, God. That was You speaking. How can anyone leave a place like this?" After much discussion with God, I needed to know when was I supposed to leave. I didn't hear another sound from heaven that day.

A year went by before I was given more instructions for my departure from Broken Arrow. When God gave me the green light to proceed, I asked my sisters in the Lord to pray and believe with me. I had less than two days to put my furniture in storage, and the pressure was on. I spoke to my sister in the Lord, Soni, about it, and her suggestion was to sell it. I said, "Do you think I can sell it all in two days?"

She and another sister bought most of it. Everything was sold within two days. Just *believe*—and see His Glory!

In 1994, I returned to Michigan. At my mother's house, the phone rang. The person on the other end was calling to get my phone number in Broken Arrow. My mother said, "You don't need her number because she's right here." She gave the phone to me.

My niece began to apologize for not getting in touch with me.

I said, "It's okay because I knew God healed your baby that day. There wasn't any doubt about that."

She said, "Thank you so much because when I took him back to the doctor, they did an echocardiogram of his heart and said, 'We don't know how, but somehow, tissue has grown over the hole. It's no longer there, and as for the Down syndrome, my baby is doing everything he wants to do."

I began to praise God like never before. I said, "I would ask God why you hadn't called me, but I know the Lord healed him." I held on to my faith and believed God's Word. "If you only believe, you can see the Glory of God" (John 11:40 KJV). It's like your Knower knows, and there is absolutely no place for doubt and unbelief.

I accepted a travel position at a medical center in an inner city. One morning, I was working in the pre-op area. I went to the surgical waiting area to get my first patient for the day, and I overheard a conversation between another patient and the nurse at the desk. The patient had read through her consent form and was going to omit what she was not going to consent to. She began to cross it out on the form.

I thought, *Lord, please do not let her be one of my patients later on*. I took my patient back to the pre-op area and prepped them for surgery. After about an hour, I noticed the patient on a stretcher in a pre-op cubicle. I was thankful that another nurse had already prepped her.

Within minutes, the Lord said, "Go tell her I love her."

I said, "Go tell her You love her?" The awful spirit of fear came upon me. I felt like I was paralyzed. I agreed to go over and say what God was telling me. I took a few steps toward her, and the fear increased. I stopped.

An intense voice said, "I said go tell her I love her."

For the third time, I agreed. I reached her stretcher, and her eyes were closed. I thought, *Yes, she's asleep! I now have a way out of doing what God asked of me.*

Her eyes opened, and any chance of getting out of it was just not happening.

I said, "Hello. How are you doing?"

She told me that she had a three-hour drive to the hospital from a college town in a rural area. She was a professor at the college.

I understood why she went over the consent form with a fine-toothed comb. I appeared calm on the outside, but on the inside, I was fighting the fear of telling her what God had sent me to say.

After a few minutes of conversation, she said, "There is nothing to do there."

I asked if there were any churches in the area. That was my opening line to do what I was asked to do. We began talking about church and God.

I told her God had sent me over to let her know that He loves her. As I shared my love for God, she saw my sincerity and asked for prayer. She shared that she had bladder cancer and a disabled husband. I felt a surge of God's healing and anointing, and I closed the curtain and began to pray.

I did what Jesus did when he prayed. "He lifted up His eyes and said, 'Father, I thank thee that thou hast heard me'" (John 11:41 KJV). I look to heaven and believe that Father God hears me when I pray. When God gave me the release, I ended the prayer. I knew He had done the work. I said, "God has healed you, and you will not have to come back to the doctor about this." I assured her that I would check on her during her post-op phase.

Hours passed, and my caseload increased. I forgot to check to see if her surgery had finished. As I went into the recovery area to get a liter of sodium chloride for another patient, she called my name. I went to her bedside, and she told me that they hadn't put her to sleep. She had received another type of anesthetic. "The doctor said they found no cancer, and I don't have to come back."

I was teary-eyed and rejoiced with her because God was doing what He does healing all manner of sickness and disease, if we believe:

> These signs shall follow them that believe, they shall lay hands on the sick, and they shall recover. (Mark 16:17, 19 KJV)
>
> The prayer of faith shall save the sick and the Lord shall raise them up. (James 5:15 KJV)
>
> The effectual fervent prayer of a righteous man or *woman* avails much. (James 5:16 KJV)

I love the Amplified Bible translation of this verse: "Makes tremendous power available dynamic in its working."

That's the dynamics of God's healing power. Several encounters with God's power at work have caused my faith to increase to the level of believing and knowing God can and will do all that we ask and believe Him for. My sword is constantly being sharpened, and I've learned to activate the power that sustains the weapon. The sword of the Spirit is the Word of God!

CHAPTER 7

You Know It's According to Your Faith

Say What You Believe: Speak the Word

In the summer of 1981, life at home with my husband was more of a challenge than I needed. *There is infidelity, and I have had enough of this emotional ride. I'm new to the faith in God and am trying my best to deal with this situation as I learn the scriptures and how to do things God's way.* Promise after promise was made that the extramarital affairs would stop, but they were just more lies. The only way I knew to deal with it was to soak myself in the things of God.

I positioned myself to five o'clock prayer every morning. I would listen to the radio broadcast of the Faith Seminar of the Air with Brother Kenneth E. Hagin, Jerry Savelle, and then R. W. Shambach. These men of God fed my spirit daily along with my pastor, Elder Isaac King Jr. I attended church services every Sunday morning and evening, along with weekly services on Tuesday and Friday nights. This was the only outlet for me to try to remain sweet, kind, and loving during those difficult times.

It was aggravating. I did not want to see his face when he came home. I knew my heart was not right toward him—and that was not of God. I thought, *If I could leave him, this would certainly help my emotions—and I can make it right in my heart again.*

Thoughts began to surface, and I started planning how I would move. I remembered a neighbor who had moved to California, and I decided to visit for what I thought would be a two-week vacation. When I got in touch and made plans to go, I mentioned it to my younger sister. She is my best friend, and I knew she would be willing to do whatever I asked. We are very close, and there is nothing we would not do for one another within the saintly duty.

All the plans were made, and I let my mother know what I was planning to do with my life. I had spent months planning, building my faith, and believing that everything would work out because I was in covenant with God, and He promised to supply all of my needs:

> If you abide in me, and My words abide in you, ye shall ask what ye will, and it shall be done unto you. (John 15:7 KJV)

I knew that I was living His Word and that He was living in me; there was no question concerning that. I believed that I could activate my faith to believe what I asked for was mine.

I was planning more than a trip to see my friends. It was a game changer. My plans no longer included returning to the small town I grew up in; it was a new life in sunny Southern California.

My mother automatically went into the fear and doubt mode. "You don't have a job out there."

I responded, "I believe that God will have one for me when I get there."

My mother said, "Your sister doesn't have a job either—and you're taking her with you?"

I said, "God will take care of us. I have faith to believe that's what will happen."

Mother insisted that I did not have a degree.

"No, I do not have a degree, Mother, but I do have God. He will not let us fail."

My beloved mother found every excuse in the book to convince me not to act on what I believed. I had developed an intimate relationship with God, and there was no doubt that jobs were waiting for us upon our arrival in Los Angeles. This story ends with a thirty-six-hour cross-country drive from Inkster, Michigan, to Los Angeles, California, with three female drivers and my firstborn son. Two of us were filled with faith in God.

Our navigation system mapped out the route. We were able to navigate through mountains with high altitudes and deserts in extreme heat. In the desert, there were certain places where running the air-conditioning was restricted because of the possibility of overheating. Being stranded in the hot desert was not an option for us.

My five-year-old son took off his clothes due to the heat and said, "Mommy, why is Jesus doing this to us?"

I said, "What is Jesus doing to us?"

He said, "Why did Jesus make it so hot?"

I had to explain to him in words he could understand about the desert being a dry place. "There is not much water, and the ground absorbs heat from that big bright sun in the sky, causing the heat to rise."

The only stops we made were for gas and to-go food. We were on a mission to achieve a goal.

We hit the California state line at one o'clock on Sunday morning. Once we reached our destination, we were totally exhausted. We vowed that if we returned home, the car would be shipped—and we'd fly back on a plane. At our friends' place, we were excited since it had been more than a decade since we'd seen them. They made room for us to stay and said that we should think about making their place home. That was our plan.

We bought a newspaper to check out the want ads to see what God had lined up for us. I was a surgical technician, and my sister's degree was in home economics. On Monday morning, we both rose early because of the time difference and decided we would find our jobs that we believed God for. One of the community hospitals was hiring, and I applied there. She saw an ad for an assistant manager for a company in her field, and she applied for that job. Within the week, we both were hired with decent salaries.

God had done just what we believed He would do: supply the need "according to His riches and glory by Christ Jesus" (Phil. 4:19 KJV). It was time to call Mother and share the good news of how faithful God is when you choose to believe Him. Mother was at peace to know that God had made a way for us to have an income, but she was not excited to know that her two youngest daughters were more than 2,200 miles away from home. God has extra special treats for you when you abide in Him.

Three of us were hired at the hospital. Two of us were in our twenties, and the other lady was a little older. One was from Ohio, one was from California, and I was from Michigan. A few weeks after we started, the anesthesiologists gave us a welcome party at an exclusive restaurant in Santa Monica. I'll never forget the size of the delicious beef ribs. I thought, *They had to have gotten these ribs from a dinosaur.* They had gifts for us and thank-you notes for helping them with their surgical procedures. *Wow,* I thought. *What love God will have others extend toward you.*

That is the only hospital I've worked at where they supplied so many treats to their employees. Every morning, the lounge was stocked with newspapers, chocolate and white milk, coffee, tea, orange juice, doughnuts, saltine crackers, graham crackers, and peanut butter. It was one big happy family, and everyone worked together with respect. God takes good care of those who will believe.

The multicultural staff worked together well and cared for their coworkers. I will never forget our charge nurse. She was one of the most loving and caring people in management. She truly loved her staff and saw to it that they were taken care of—and the doctors were just as nice. There was no separation of titles there. The doctors, nurses, surgical technicians, environmental technicians, transporters, clerks, and supervisors all shared the lounge.

I felt culture shock when I saw so many different cultures coming together, getting along, and talking with no hidden agendas. The place I left in Michigan was not that way. There was one majority of people, and there was little communication among the people who did not look like each other. I knew I was in the right place to experience these one-of-a-kind relationships. I believed God would take care of us there, and that is exactly what He did. He is faithful to His Word.

Within weeks, my sister and I were settled in our own place in Hawthorne. Everything we believed God for had happened. We were living the dream. It actually came true as babes in Christ. It was like being told by your parents that you would get a bicycle for

Christmas—and you simply took them at their word. When that special day comes, there is the promise right before your eyes.

God's Word is surer than our parents' words are. When we believe what He says, it shall come to pass. We said, "Mother, God will take care of us and supply the need."

My desire was to live comfortable in a nice area there in California. "Delight thyself in the Lord; and He shall give thee the desire of thine heart" (Psalm 37:4 KJV).

Before long, we had furnished our townhouse. We looked around, smiled, and screamed, "Isn't God good? Wow! And Mother didn't believe with us." We learned to trust Him for everything no matter how small it seemed. We knew God was concerned about His daughters.

Looking to Jesus

We began attending one of the largest churches there in Los Angeles; we experienced the Lord's presence there and enjoyed the fellowship of believers. The choir was off the Richter scale when it came to praise and worship. The gifts and talents among the voices were truly amazing. I will never forget one of the songs that blessed my soul and stirred something up on the inside of me. The song was "Look to Jesus."

That was a turning point for me. No matter what happened, what someone said or did, or how they appeared to be, I would look to Jesus. We can learn how to not get worked up about things that are out of our control or negative situations brought about by others—and be assured that it is not worth losing your anointing over. I often say, "When you enter the house of worship, your focus is God. Allow the Holy Spirit to speak as He reveals Jesus to you."

There never will be a perfect house of worship long as there are imperfect people in attendance. I know of too many believers who have been damaged by "church folk" and have almost totally dismissed God because of being hurt. They do not attend worship service anymore, and some have vowed to never set foot in a church building again. My heart is saddened when I hear such things. For one, it was not the person who inflicted the wound who called you to purpose and destiny, established a covenant with you, or created you with a lifetime assignment that's larger that yourself to reach others through the power of His Word.

> This is not the time to pull away and neglect meeting together, as some have formed the habit of doing. In fact, we should come together even more frequently, eager to encourage and urge each other onward as we anticipate that day dawning. (Hebrews 10:25 TPT)

When others share their painful experiences with me, I offer words of encouragement, mention how Jesus died for them, and remind them that Jesus is the reason for all seasons. When we look to Jesus, we relive the awesome experience of His love and faithfulness toward us. We forget all about what was done to us by others.

There are times when believers forget who they are and who they belong to, and they yield to the enemy. The Bible teaches us about the enemy's cunning and craftiness when he entices someone who knows what God has said, yet they will succumb to the temptation that opposes the Word of the Lord.

So many examples in the Word of God teach us what happens when we yield our members to satanic spirits. Adam fell from grace, and sin entered. Lot's wife turned into a pillar of salt, Moses didn't enter into promise land, and King Josiah lost his life in a battle that God didn't give him to fight. There are many more stories to tell. When we focus on God calling us, we enter a place of purpose and walk out the destiny of His grace.

One of the most important stances to take is to know that God will get His Word to you right when you need to hear it—if you listen to Him. He has your back, and no weapon of any kind will thrive or flourish against you because you are in covenant with the King of glory! He is the King of kings. No matter where the attack is coming from, God's plan for your life shall blossom.

In a church I was a member of, we facilitated discipleship classes where people's lives were literally changed. Their purpose was revealed, and they were adamant about fulfilling what God had called them to do. During the twelfth week of the fourteen-week appointment with God, it was pressed upon our hearts to have an all-night prayer shut-in with God during our forty-day consecration. It was approved by the pastor and the First Lady.

When the pastor and the First Lady went on vacation, two of the associate female ministers allowed the spirit of opposition to infiltrate their spirits to try to stop the shut-in. When it was mentioned to me, I immediately wanted to find out more information. The so-called mastermind behind the issue convinced the other one to do the devil's work for her. I asked why it was happening. The ambiguous and confusing answer didn't make sense to me, and I chose to wait and look to the Lord for help.

I spoke to God about it and decided that I would not interrupt the pastor and the First Lady's vacation. I spoke to my heavenly Father, and I knew that He had answered my prayer. His favor was given to us. They were scheduled to return by the end of the week, and the issue could be addressed then.

When I spoke to the First Lady, she said, "Loretta, just act like that conversation never happened. I will speak to the pastor and call you right back."

I thanked her and hung up the phone.

Within a few minutes, that she returned the call and said, "You all can have your prayer shut-in on Friday night. Use the commercial kitchen for your breakfast in the morning—and we have provided security for you all night long." That is what happens when you choose not to fight your battles and allow Holy Spirit to lead you and guide you.

On Friday night, we gathered with prayer. The women in leadership brought the Word of the Lord, and I strongly support allowing believers to operate in their anointing. Never hinder what God has deposited into others by suppressing or holding them back from ministering because of your insecurities. They each spoke powerful words, and the holy presence of God filled the place. I remember the healings that took place that night. A sister had been suffering from multiple sclerosis and hadn't been able to walk without a walker or cane—and she walked around the huge sanctuary that night without any assistance. I walked slowly behind her the entire way, and her gait was steady as can be.

One of the ministers saw angelic beings flying around the sanctuary. A prophetic utterance was given to bless the women of God.

When we look to God in the name of Jesus, we experience the manifestation of His glory. We were on one accord in our fasting and consecrations to the Lord. For twelve weeks, we had been seeking the face of God and desiring to meet with Him. That time of prayer, worship, praise, and operating in faith created an atmosphere that was conducive for the Holy Spirit to enter and do what only He can do. He can heal the sick, speak the Word through yielded vessels to Him, and change lives for His glory. Everything we believed God for happened that night, and it was because of our faith that those awesome things occurred for us!

Work It, Jesus. Work It!

I was brought up under the tender spiritual care of church mothers who taught me how to live in a holy and righteous way in this present world. Some were bound in tradition, and others knew how to be free in the Spirit. Years later, our church mother was replaced by another person under circumstances that were not understood by most. It happened, and we accepted the change, but most of the women still referred to our mother emeritus and assistant mothers when they needed guidance and council.

The three church mothers remained faithful to what God had called them to do with love, love, and more love. I will always remember them as the most loving people I have ever seen serving the Lord. It taught me so much about how to love the unlovely, the rebellious, the contrary, and those who try to use and abuse you.

On weeknights, we would have one service with two different sessions. During the first session, the church mother would have the missionaries bring a short message to the church. She would avoid asking me because I did not hold the same license as the other missionaries. I was licensed under the leadership of the late Kenneth E. Hagin, and because I was not licensed under who she thought I should be, she purposely saw to it that I would not speak on Tuesday nights. It was perfectly all right with me because the pastor would call me to speak on Sunday nights, and sometimes it was in the spur of the moment.

The head deacon would come to where I was sitting and say, "The pastor wants to know if you would bring the Word tonight."

I was taught in Bible school to always be ready: "Be ye also ready" (Matthew 24:44 KJV). I always kept a prepared message handy in my Bible in case that occurred.

On a Tuesday night, the church mother addressed the congregation after the final message. She decided to throw darts while hiding her hands. Everyone who was in hearing distance knew that she was taking shots at me. They slowly began to look my way with shock on their faces. "If a person is not licensed by this denomination, then they can't carry the title. I have not seen any license—so how I would know if there are any?" One by one, the women in the service began to laugh because they could not believe it was happening with the pastor sitting right up front in the pulpit.

A sister turned around and said, "Do you know she's talking about you?"

I smiled, nodded, and maintained a loving composure. I knew God would handle it. I said, "Daddy's got this." I believe in looking to Jesus. He governs well. He has control over this, and He has everything in check.

The pastor had seen my license and accepted it as if I was confirmed by the denomination. Upon completion of her radical ramblings, the pastor got up behind her and said, "If I send my son and daughter to a Bible school, and they both study for the ministry, my daughter will probably do better with her grades. They both graduate and return home to the church, and you say that my son can preach, but she can't? There is no way you are going to tell me I can license my son but not my daughter. She spent just as much time in school as he did, and you are trying to tell me she can't preach? Not so, not so! She speaks better than my son. Not so, not so."

It was as if her balloon had exploded, her tomato was squashed, and the nitrogen pressure was released from the line. She squirmed in the seat. My God. The amen corner was activated, and the "praise the Lords" got stronger. I rejoiced in the One I knew to release this situation to. As a popular song says, "While you're trying to figure it out, Jesus has already worked it out." I knew God was working on my behalf and that He would answer, but I didn't realize it would be that soon. Patience is a virtue, and love is powerful. When we operate in both, the shaking of the enemy's camp will dismantle it.

After the service, we greeted each other in the saint's manner.

When I reached the parking lot, the sisters said, "She never expected that, did she, sister?" "She never knew that the pastor would come to your defense so quick." "Did you see her in that chair?"

I said, "God is great and greatly to be praised." I had to remain steadfast in faith. I knew that God was working on my behalf to blanket this flame, which had been simmering for quite some time. When you notice that sparks are flying, the flame will eventually cause a fire to erupt. That is when prayer is your ammunition. "Effectual fervent prayer makes tremendous power available dynamic in its working" (James 5:16 AMP). The Holy Spirit will guide you about how to respond with His love.

> We know that all things work together for good to them that love God, to them who are the called according to His purpose. (Romans 8:28 KJV)

It's just something you should know, be familiar with, have deposited within your spirit, understand as truth, and have it established and soundly settled in your heart.

I love God with all my heart, and those who truly know me strongly agree that my love for Him goes to the deepest chamber of my spirit. God's Word is alive! When an attack is dispersed from the enemy, the Word of God on the inside of you is activated—and life in His Word catapults you with supernatural power. Faith is the activator that triggers the power inside of you. The Apostle Paul wrote, "Fight the good fight of faith." This is the only fight that God allows us to fight (1 Timothy 6:12 KJV).

The battle is never ours to fight; it's the Lord's. God is faithful to His Word of promise, which is reliable to the finish:

> Retribution and the deliverance of justice rest with Me. I will repay the wrongdoer. The Lord will judge His people. (Hebrews 10:30 AMP)

Judgment comes swiftly, and I'm always amazed at what God does on our behalf when we are found in the right place.

The Bible says, "Faith is" (Hebrews 11:1 KJV), which is present tense. That means, right now, faith gets the attention of the

Father, and heaven releases the answer, the plan, the strategy, the healing, the vindication, the timing, or whatever else is needed on our behalf.

The Holy Spirit lives on the inside of every Spirit-filled born-again believer, and He speaks to our spirit all day and every day. God's Word clearly says to the believer, "He that has ears to hear, let him hear" (Matthew 11:15 KJV). "Anyone with ears to hear should listen and understand" (NLT). "He that hath an ear, let him hear what the Spirit God says unto the churches" (Revelation 2:29 KJV).

Are you the church? If so, then He is speaking to you. As people of God, we tend to not tune in to spiritual things, especially when we think we know something or have a small amount of knowledge on a particular subject.

There are times when we think we are smarter than God. We make decisions, and we consult other people even when we know they do not know the Lord. For some reason, God is the last resort for gaining insight into what we need answers to. He knows all things, and He had the plan mapped out before the foundation of the world. He knows the end from the beginning, sits high, looks low, and answers before you ask.

> According as His divine power has given unto us all things that pertain unto life and godliness, through the knowledge of Him that has called us by glory and virtue. (2 Peter 1:3 KJV)

The key insight is that "it's *through* the knowledge of Him." He has called you to glory and virtue. A place of dignity, honor, and splendor results in the praise and glory of who He is. Abiding in the knowledge of Him will bring us to a place of moral excellence, greatness, and perfection.

Well, you might think that no one will ever be perfect—no matter how hard we try. That is true if you are thinking along the lines of someone never making a mistake or missing the mark. Being in this human suit, we will miss the mark at times, but we have been covered for that:

> If we confess our sins, He is faithful and just to forgive us our sins, and to cleanse us from all unrighteousness. (1 John 1:9 KJV)

We should not make a habit of purposefully living without spiritual boundaries.

As Jesus was teaching a lesson to His disciples and revealing to them the endless possibility to operate in love, He covered every opportunity to perfect them. To end the lesson, He said, "Be ye therefore perfect, even as your Father which is in heaven is perfect" (Matthew 5:48 KJV).

Perfection simply means being mature. God expects us to grow up naturally and spiritually in this life. He starts us off with the sincere milk of the Word, and then He expects us to take hold of the meat of the Word. As we mature in the spiritual realm, we experience the workings of the Holy Spirit. Would not He do it? Yes, He will work it out.

CHAPTER 8

No Issues in My Tissues

Hidden Within

The Bible has answers for every situation we encounter in life. Life is filled with surprises, laughter, disappointment, pain, and frustration to mention a few. There are times when what we think is the best solution for any given situation can be interrupted or intercepted by another person or thing. It is not an easy task to remain calm through trying times when someone else enters our space without being invited to do so. This happens in the home or workplace, in relationship, and in conversations where decisions have to be made. These moments of sheer aggravation cause irritability within the soulish realm, which activates the caged gorilla that's lying dormant because nothing has triggered a spark.

When pressed beyond a boiling point by circumstances that are not part of the agreement, something on the inside erupts like a volcano. The emotional lava supersedes its boundary, and we find ourselves saying and doing what we believed was no longer a part of our being. Yes, there will be times of testing by people and incidents that take us by surprise.

It would be wonderful if we walked super spiritually twenty-four hours a day and were able to avoid certain plights. Predicaments we encounter daily distract our focus from what could easily prevent most negative situations—even when we know scripture instructs us to "walk not after the flesh, but after the Spirit" (Romans 8:1 KJV). God understands that we operate in the natural realm as well, and this is where most challenges occur. This gives us the freedom to apply that which we know to put into action what we "say" we believe.

This opportunity of yielding to the Spirit of God positions us in the scope that allows Him to work on our behalf. God is always engaged in favoring those whose lives are hidden in Him. There is a divine connection between God and the ones who are hidden in Him. You must see Him as the go-between in any test or trial you experience. The outcome shall increase your faith, allow intimacy in His presence through prayer, and maintain an established relationship that's inseparable. Each time you are willing to believe and trust Him to take the lead, the amazing results will inspire you to become more acquainted with Him.

It illuminates our spirit to come alive in Him. Being hidden in Christ is like being held secretly from the hand of opposing forces. When the enemy sanctions his imps to attack God's precious loved ones, he has to obtain permission, and he has to try to find out where they are because he does not know all things.

God has ordained each person an assignment to be fulfilled on this earth with a certain time and season upon which it activates. The anointing that causes us to be hidden in Christ is a concealing factor. We have been given instructions and are equipped with spiritual gear to handle the assignment with victory. The enemy wants us to believe that he is more powerful than God and that he is omnipresent. Not so. Not so. The devil is a created being just as we are, and the only power he has is that which we yield and hand over to him. He was defeated at Calvary and when Jesus conquered death, hell, and the grave, it was done.

The elders conjured up the lie to say that "Jesus's disciples came by night and stole Him away while they slept" (Matthew 28:13 KJV). Jesus walked out of the grave and instructed His disciples to come to the mountain in Galilee:

> All power is given unto me in heaven and in earth. Go ye therefore, and teach all nations baptizing them in the name of the Father, and of the Son, and of the Holy Ghost: Teaching them to observe all things

> whatsoever I have commanded you: and, lo, I am with you always, even unto the end of the world. Amen. (Matthew 28:18–20 KJV)

I believe that I am in the "all nations" He was referring to. It wasn't just Israel, Turkey, Anatolia, Asia Minor, and other Middle Eastern nations. On another occasion, He said, "Go ye into all the world" (Mark 16:15 KJV). The United States is a nation, and the same power that caused Jesus to rise from the dead abides in us if we are truly hidden in Him.

> And if the Spirit of Him who raised Jesus from the dead lives in you, He who raised Christ Jesus from the dead will also give life to your mortal bodies through His Spirit, who lives in you. (Romans 8:11 AMP)

Bless His holy name! He lives in me.

Offense? What's That?

When things happen that are not in the agreement, life can take a turn. At times, you can find yourself tied in a loop. I recall a situation where I had given my all to help a relative who was dying from cancer. I left a great-paying job to help take care of them and even went as far as to cash in one of my 401(k) accounts, which allowed me the privilege of not working for several months so I could be there to help provide comfort and make things a litter easier for him.

As a registered nurse with years of experience, I assisted him in every way possible: talking with the doctors, checking lab values, making sure the medications were taken correctly, checking infections, helping steady his gait, traveling to doctor appointments three or four times a week, and supporting him spiritually. He had witnessed God's power of healing anointing before and knew that God is yet on His throne, doing what only He can do.

I received a call from him at three o'clock one morning, and he asked if I could take him to the hospital because he couldn't urinate even though he had a urinary catheter in place. He had been trying to urinate for two hours, but nothing would come out. I asked, "Where are you?"

He said, "On my way to your house."

I got out of bed and prepared myself to take him to the hospital. As soon as the doorbell rang, I let him in. With God is my witness, as I stood by the sofa table, allowing him to go into the kitchen, he brushed against me. As soon as he entered the kitchen, the urine came running down into his leg bag. He said, "I have been up walking through the house trying to get this urine out of me for hours, and it wouldn't come out. I get over here, and it flows right out."

I looked at him and said, "You better recognize the anointing when you see it."

He nodded and said, "I guess so."

That morning, God delivered him from what could have been an additional health concern and saved him the expense of going to the emergency room. To my amazement, this did not change his behavior. He suffered miserably and could have received his divine healing just by obeying God. His sinful sexual appetite ruled his life, and Satan had such a tenacious grip on him with infidelity in two different marriages, and he was not willing to deal with it:

> Choosing rather to suffer with the people of God than to enjoy the pleasures of sin for a season. (Hebrews 11:25 KJV)

Sin is only enjoyed for a season, and then all hell breaks loose. The choice is ours even though God has given His Word and instructions on how to escape the works of the enemy. God gave us the power of choice in the Garden of Eden. Everything was provided and given to Adam with understanding of the choices he would make. When we stop using the power that resides in our spirit man, we tend to fall prey to the enemy of our soul, allowing that issue to remain in our tissues.

His sister was diagnosed with ovarian cancer and was at the point of giving in to the cancer until I was led to visit her at the hospital. I brought a book about healing: *God's Creative Power for Healing*.

Sharing God's Word requires our faith in action. As I prayed and laid hands on her, the power of God entered that room. In faith, she took hold of His presence and received her healing that day. God led me to pray for her in a soft voice. I commanded cancer to leave her body and every cancer cell to be destroyed in the name of Jesus. Prior to praying, I reminded her that God was in charge of her life and that the devil had no place in her or near her.

We have been made aware that "the thief comes to steal, kill, and destroy, but Jesus came that she may have life and life abundantly" (John 10:10 KJV). I poured God's Word into her spirit like a massive construction site. I purposed to have every Word of God settled in her without any doubt. When we pray, that is the time to believe what we say. The mixing of faith with the Word of God stirs the power of God, which creates the manifestation to receive what has already been given to us.

As I prayed, tears streamed down her face. The power of God come upon her, and she began to feel and sense His presence in the hospital room. She said, "I felt a lot of heat over my body when you touched me, and I never knew that anyone could pray as gently and soft as you did—and that God would hear them and come in. I have always heard people praying loud as if God could not hear them unless they were talking at a high volume. I have truly learned something today from this."

I said, "Yes, God hears us when we activate our faith to believe what He said in His Word."

The difference between these two siblings is that she was a believer and lived the life of a true faithful Christian. God gifted her as a musician, and when she worshipped the Lord, you could not contain yourself. You were not just a spectator; you were participating in the presence of the Lord. What the devil wanted to do was silence her praise. He wanted to stop the flow of God's anointing upon those present when she would minister in music.

God had opened door after door for her to minister in song and music across this nation. Before her illness, she would visit her parents and play the organ. We would experience a high time in the Lord. Her worship over all the years was stored up for the day when God would supernaturally come in and touch her body with His healing hand to remove the cancer. It could not stay because she belonged to Him, and He was not finished with her.

Her time of departure had not come. We refused to allow the imp to set up camp on territory that did not belong to him. The issue in her tissue began in 2000, and God's healing saturated her body in 2001. In 2020, she is still healed and free of cancer. I want to stop here and praise Him!

> Ringing in the new year of 2001, I discovered that my mission was have faith and trust God as I never had done before. Ever. This body that God loaned me housed cancer in an ovary that remained from my surgery in 1996. As this mission progressed, God worked in my husband's favor. Derwin was to be a guideline for me. On the inspirational side, I was to receive prayers, inspirational words, and songs. From that point on, the blessings of the Lord poured in.
>
> On this mission, I faced various challenges. My guardians, friends, parents, and siblings became evidence of God's orchestration in this mission for me. Its purpose was to get to know God for myself. I witnessed more knowledge about prayer and the way people pray. This is still in my spirit to this day. The spouse of my eldest sibling, Loretta, was commissioned to lay her hand across my stomach with a book by Charles Capps: *God's Creative Power for Healing*.
>
> I had been vomiting for a while and needed a tube to be placed inside. Being unbearable and uncomfortable, I was in need of a miracle. It felt like God had made an assembly line within my body with warmth, noises, and good feelings. You see, Loretta laid hands on me and prayed in a soft voice. I knew she was praying. For a bit of humor, I now know that God is not deaf, as I thought before. In closing, this mission is about God's healing and His own time on His own terms, and however this turned out for me, I'm grateful. I'm still alive in 2020. Regardless of your feelings, it's all about God. Always.

Two different situations illustrate Satan's attack on the body with sickness and disease. Disease brings upon us a sense of dis-ease, feeling disconnected from that which we know God has given us through the power of His Word. If we maintain our gaze on Him, feeding on His Word—because it is medicine—we will experience God's powerful result. "Health to all of our flesh" (Proverbs 4:22 KJV).

There are reasons that some do not receive their healing. There is nothing wrong with God, His Word, or His power. It is according to our faith, be it unto us (Matthew 9:29 KJV). We choose how we react to situations. We can either acknowledge that this one is for God, activate our faith like never before, and believe that Father God is true to his Word—or we can succumb to it and allow Satan to continually lie to us. The latter is contrary to the Word of God. If that were true, then God would be working with the devil—and we know that is a lie.

How often do we search our hearts to see if we're holding on to unforgiveness against someone in the past who has truly harmed us? How often do we begin a spiritual probe within us by checking our love walk toward one another? Do we examine our lifestyles to see if it lines up with what's written in God's Word? Are we caught in the enemy's web of ungodly relationships or engaged in sexual sin? Yes, the enemy has lured Christians into straddling the fence because of living so close to the edge and ignoring the fact that we are no longer bound. We have stepped athwart the line of demarcation.

When sickness is allowed entrance into our bodies, there is an uproar of emotion that may not line up with the Word of God on how to launch an attack from a fleshly stance. We feel like we have been wronged or are being persecuted. We plan an attack on the source of the invasion. I have heard people say, "God allowed this sickness to come to teach me a lesson." They believe that this justifies blaming God for what He does not do. "He sent His word, and healed them, and delivered them from their destructions" (Psalm 107:20 KJV).

We compare our works and deeds to advocate our own cases and fail to realize that going to church and living a God-fearing life are two different perspectives. I believe that a door has opened, and the enemy is granted entrance into our lives. God only allows what we allow. He's given us power with authority to defeat the devil when His Word is mixed with our faith: "According to your faith be it unto you" (Matthew 9:29 KJV).

Jesus touched the blind men who followed him after hearing of a certain ruler's dead daughter. Jesus laid his hand on her and assured them that she was not dead; she was sleeping. After being ridiculed and laughed at, Jesus continued showing forth God's power.

No matter how opposing forces try to go against what you know is true, do not become distracted or diverted. Keep your spotlight focused on His Word. Doubt and unbelief are to be cast out of your spirit and handled. Faith takes the forefront. You must take a stand and know what you believe in. One can only imagine that the praise was so overwhelming that people were talking about it for days throughout the region. "Faith comes by hearing" (Romans 10:17 KJV).

The two blind men had their hearing senses in active status, which enabled them to assign their faith in full capacity to believe that if Jesus would have mercy on them, they would receive their sight. They asked Jesus for mercy, and He said, "Do you believe that I am able to do this?" Their mouths were lined up with what was in their hearts. "Yes, Lord" (Matthew 9:29 KJV).

God is waiting to hear these words: "Yes, Lord." I am so thankful that I grew up in a church that taught us to say yes to the Lord. We sang a song back then, and I still sing it to God. Two simple words, "Yes, Lord," should be our answer to all of God's commands, plans, and instructions for our lives.

The blind men did not physically see the maid in the house raised from the dead. Their faith was increased when they began to hear the report of what happened when Jesus showed up. The Bible talks about how the fame spread all across the region. The blind men could not see a thing, yet they put their faith to work based on what they heard others talking about. Their minds were made up to receive what they believed. Faith comes by hearing the Word of God. The word on the street was "Jesus heals," which they heard, and because of their faith, there were no longer any "issues in their tissues."

God Quietly Removes Issues

In 2014, I chose not to offer my services to someone who had been living a double life filtered with lying, cheating, and disgrace to the body of Christ. I had just returned from a missionary trip in

Africa. While I was there, his father passed away. I decided to go by to check on him. By that time, we were living in separate homes due to the fact that he wasn't able to get his life together. I decided when I was a teenager that I would never share a man. That is not God's will for anyone.

I believe that, and I lived it. I vowed to be true no matter what the other person did or did not do. When I made the decision to go over there, there was a check in my spirit, an unction from the Holy Spirit not to go. Allowing my flesh to kick in, I overrode His lead. I wanted to know why the Holy Spirit was leading me not to go. There is never a time to override God's lead. His leadings are always the path to travel.

When we choose to disobey, we defy spiritual authority. Our actions speak for us. It infringes on the benefit God has ordained. When we find ourselves caught up in situations that were never a part of His plan or promise, God will "also make a way to escape" (1 Corinthians 10:13 KJV). This will protect us from utter disaster. If I had listened to God, this issue would not have saturated in my tissues.

As I parked the car, I notice two women heading to the door. One tried to explain that they were "bringing some food," but that wasn't necessary knowing his history and that she was willing to do whatever he wanted. We all entered the house and began to engage in a conversation about the mission trip. To his surprise, the other lady and I had established a relationship years ago—and there was no matter of contention with each other.

The time together turned out to be fruitful, sharing the mission work seem to interest them. His perspiration stopped once he realized that the conversation was not about him. After a couple of hours, the two of them left. We were left alone to talk. I asked why he did not let me know that his father had passed. I mentioned that I had received a text in Africa from another person. He showed me his phone. It was on the phone I used for ministry, and I had not seen it.

After about an hour, he began to lie about not feeling well. He said he wanted to lie down and rest. I knew he was not speaking truthfully and suggested that he go ahead and lie down. I would be in the kitchen if he needed something. The conversation went back and forth for several minutes, and there was a knock at the door. He heard it, but he refused to answer it.

After several knocks, I said, "Why are you not answering the door?"

He stared at me in silence. I said, "If you won't, I will." I opened the door saw the concubine who he had been cheating with for several years. We exchanged a few words, and she brushed against me as she came in. I quickly regained my space.

It didn't matter that she was there because I was so over it—and him. God will give us the peace we need when our minds are focused upon Him. I wanted him to know that he could no longer hide behind his lying spirit. He was looking like a sick puppy that desperately needed help from God.

She convinced him to call the police and send them to my home with a lie that they wanted to speak to me about. I did not answer the door and chose to not deal with it until I spoke with my attorney. They sent registered mail to my address, but I refused to open it. Weeks later, I mentioned it to my attorney, and he suggested that I open it and read it. He had placed a PPO on me so that I couldn't be near him.

This frustrated me. I had helped take care of him for eighteen months! Yes, the flesh began to take charge, and every emotion known to women surfaced. The caged gorilla began to bend the bars to escape. Yielding to the flesh is an indicator that we are taking things into our own hands and denying God access to work through things.

I allowed insensitivity and retaliation in, and I began to feel such hatred for him. I was at the point where it did not matter whether he lived or died. That was the state of my heart during that time. Yes, I was still a born-again Bible believer and an anointed child of the King. Was God still using me? Yes, He was. Was He still speaking to me through his Word and prophetic voice? Yes, He was. Did He ever give up on me? No, He did not because of the plan He ordained for me before I ever came to be was established before the foundation of the world.

There was a war between my spirit and my flesh. I called on God every day to speak to me. This situation took place for three months. There was a change in my monthly budget now that I had to pay attorney fees, and it was costly. I decided that he had created this situation and that he should be the one to foot the attorney's charges.

I was still wearing my wedding ring and another one he had bought me in another country while cruising, which I called my KB ring. He saw it in the case at the store, and it was identical to a

"Princess Di" ring. It was not as expensive as the one that had been purchased for her. He showed it to me, knowing that I would love it, and I did. He said, "If I buy this for you, will you agree that you will not bring up another concubine's name again?" He had an affair with another woman at the church we attended, and God exposed it. He had a serious problem with sexual sin.

I agreed to not bring up her name, and when he made the purchase, the salesman said, "If someone asks you about this ring, tell them it's a four-carat sapphire surrounded in diamonds set in platinum, baby!" I smiled at the man with the encouraging words. If only there was a fly on the wall to hear the conversation prior to this purchase. I wore the ring to dinner, and our friends said, "Loretta, you stole Princess Diana's ring."

That statement made me aware of her ring. I loved her, but I had not paid much attention to her ring. I gave more appreciation to the ring. I explained that he had purchased it earlier that day, and I was more excited to have it now.

My monthly budget had to be adjusted by thousands of dollars that were not allotted for in the ledger, and the two rings were worth more than twenty thousand dollars, which would be the answer for this new issue. If I had followed the Holy Spirit's leading the day I returned from Africa, maybe it would not have been a problem.

For three months, I allowed bitter feelings to harbor in my heart. I literally did not want to hear his name. He made his transition during the latter part of that year. I was so numb that it did not faze me one way or the other. People I didn't recognize would ask if I was so-and-so's wife, and I would act like they were crazy and sometimes avoid answering. This went on for about three years after his death. I knew that what I felt was not of God and that I needed to do something about it. The sad part was that I could not do a thing about it.

I knew that was not who I was, and it was overbearing to my character. I had never allowed that kind of spirit to live within me. I had always been quick to forgive because I always wanted to be forgiven by God when I needed to be. I purposed to walk in love no matter how I was treated. I made a promise to always remember that I would never be held accountable for how people treated me—only for my responses and how I treat them. I love God more than anything in this world, and I will always go to Him in prayer.

I do not know what when or where God smoothed things over for me. When it came to this man, God knew I was not operating in the love walk that I normally lived and preached about. I struggled with hearing his name or anything about him. It was an issue that I could not shake for years. I realized I was no match for what had infected my spirit. I knew it was not the Spirit of God abiding and working through me, yet I never asked God to remove this spiritual infection. It is God's will that we prosper in spirit, soul, and body.

> Beloved, I pray that in every way you may succeed and prosper and be in good health [physically], just as [I know] your soul prospers [spiritually]. (3 John 1:2 AMP)

God will intervene and help restore us to the place He wants us to be. God loves us so much, and I just realized one day that I no longer housed those terrible feelings of betrayal. He lied to me, and I was so close to feeling hatred for him. It had been removed from my heart supernaturally by the working of the Holy Spirit. It was miraculous that I have no account of a day or time that it occurred. All I know is it was God.

I was going about my tasks as usual, and I thought of him. I smiled and then laughed. I knew something had happened on the inside. I had been redeemed and renewed by God's power without asking for it. It was His amazing grace. Wow! I'd been cleansed from that nasty infection in my spirit, which caused me to act in unseemly ways toward someone who was no longer there—while the enemy was purposefully trying to hold me captive.

> "Greater is He that is within me than he that is in the world." (1 John 4:4 KJV)

God said, "Not so—this is my daughter!" God did not want me to be held captive by an antagonizing spirit that was not of Him. That day, I learned how much God really loves me. He did for me that which I hadn't asked for or prayed about. It was a day of great rejoicing. I knew in my spirit that I needed to be delivered. Thank God! I could truly say, "There are no issues in my tissues!"

CHAPTER 9

Study to be Sturdy

We must learn God's Word. "Study to show yourself approved unto God, a workman that need not to be ashamed, rightly dividing the word of truth" (1 Timothy 2:15 KJV).

Some believers read the Bible, some glance at it on Sunday mornings during worship services, and others diligently study to gain insights and deeper understanding. Studying requires more in-depth time and resources to receive revelations and visions for spiritual interpretations, which involves incorporating spiritual discipline into the study time.

At times, you will have to quiet yourself, pray things out, and wait before the Lord for clarification, inspiration, and wisdom. This does not happen in the five-second prayer time with the Father, the quick prayer in the shower, or the microwave popcorn prayer just before going to sleep. Prayer have to be developed, understood, and practiced until it becomes a lifestyle. Prayer should be second nature to a believer.

When life takes an unexpected turn, the first thing to do is pray. Nothing ever surprises God, but it might surprise you. When you study God's Word, what's been deposited into your spirit will ring loud in your inner being and direct your steps. We must sharpen our hearing to distinguish the voice of God from that of the enemy. It takes time in His presence to learn His language and hear from within.

There will be times when He speaks to you in a soft, still voice. Sometimes it will be an impression of His presence guiding you, and at other times, He will speak in an audible voice. God's direction will always grace you with His peace and comfort. There is a knowing in your spirit that senses the supernatural presence of God through the power of prayer, praise, and worship. We must know the voice of God.

Do not think for one minute that Satan is not trying to take you in the opposite direction. There are times when your thoughts play a part, and the flesh wants to do what it thinks is the answer. The scripture says to "keep our body under subjection" (1 Corinthians 9:27 KJV). You may ask, "Subjection to what?" It is subject to your spirit man. When your spirit man is in charge of your life, "we walk not after the flesh, but after the Spirit" (Romans 8:1 KJV). That's the Spirit of the Living God.

It's evident who's in charge by the life responses we release during trying times. If love radiates from our hearts when we truly have been mistreated or harmed, then we're assured of the outcome because it's not our place to retaliate. It's our place to speak the Word, pray, and believe God has our backs. The armor only protects the front portion.

> So shall my word be that goes forth out of my mouth
> it shall not return to Me void, but it shall accomplish
> that which I please, and prosper in the thing whereto
> I sent it. (Isaiah 55:11 KJV)

This is one of the most powerful verses in the Bible, and it speaks volumes about who He is. God is not a man, and He cannot lie.

Whatever God said, it is so! You can take that to the bank. When life's cares bring distraught and turbulence to your world, stir up the gift that is in you. Say what God says and triumph in His victory. He will never be defeated. The only fight we battle in is the fight of faith. Faith is the substance we grip and never let go of when we see the evidence of what was not: the thing not seen. Faith simply believes God. Never doubt—no matter how things appear to be.

When we take note of how big God is and how small our problems are to Him, we can walk this road and not fret. We should never get worked up about any situation when we have a relationship with the power of heaven abiding on the inside of us. Why carry a heavy load when Jesus wants us to cast all our cares on him? It takes hearing the Word, studying the Word, meditating on the Word, and rightly dividing the Word:

> Neither have I gone back from the commandment of his lips; I have esteemed the words of his mouth more than my necessary food. (Job 23:12 KJV)

This is how one becomes skilled in the use of the "sword of the Spirit, which is the Word of God."

Every believer can be an accomplished, competent, and seasoned user who applies the sharpest double-edged sword to reign in this life. When we understand the subject matter of who is speaking. to whom they are speaking, the why, when, and where of the text, we can apply the sword with amazing results. Other voices can influence our studies, but spiritual perception should dominate sensory perception.

> Study to show yourself approved unto God, a workman that need not to be ashamed, rightly dividing the word of truth. (2 Timothy 2:15 KJV)

Some people will put their own spin on scripture and use it to lure and deceive many others. In the past, thousands of lives were destroyed and taken because of a satanic agenda. We know the devil is behind the deception. His job is to kill, steal, and destroy (John 10:10 KJV). It's unfortunate that people will blame God when tragedy hits. They are angry with the One who created them and loves them more than anyone else because the Bible has not been studied. It's not studied when it's rarely opened.

This verse is not a suggestion; it's a command with benefits. Scripture prepares us to be ready for whatever occurs in life. There is a word from God in every encounter we experience. He wants us to know His Word, use His Word, live His Word, love His Word, and reap the results of His Word.

Knowledge of God's Word blended with faith can heal nations:

> Go ye therefore, and teach all nations: baptizing them in the name of the Father, and of the Son, and of the Holy Ghost: Teaching them to observe all things whatsoever I have commanded you: and, lo, I am with you always, even to the end of the world. Amen. (Matthew 28:19–20 KJV)

We can only teach others when we've studied the principles of the kingdom. The written Word of God is our Bible, and the Living Word of God is Jesus. Why not study Him? He and the written Word are one. God's Word enables us to comprehend who Jesus is, and that is how swords are sharpened. It is a double-bladed sword, and when it's used properly, the enemy doesn't stand a chance.

The centurion spoke to Jesus and said, "Just speak the Word only, and my servant will be healed" (Matthew 8:8 KJV). He was speaking as a man of authority who understood the principles. He knew that the words of Jesus commanded authority over sickness and disease. When we study, that's ammunition to exert that same authority. Jesus went on to say that "greater works shall you do" because He was going back to glory.

This truth was established at the creation of humanity and was expected to be produced in the lives of those whose lives are hidden in Christ. When applied foundational principles are active, the results are prodigious. Daniel's experience in the lion's den, the healing of the lame man at the temple gate—whom God raised up to not only walk but run—and Paul's healing from the venomous snake validate the greater works Jesus was speaking about. Three different men during three different occasions were operating in the power of God. They each were able to handle these encounters with savoir faire. It is written in Daniel that "the people that do know their God shall be strong and do exploits." Are you one of those people?

We can come to know God by studying His Word. After all, God and His Word are one. By spending time in His presence, praying, and giving, we fully commit to him. It is an exciting experience to know the Creator is responsible for our being here. Without God, "ye can do nothing" (John 15:5 KJV). God breathes the breath of life into us. God supplies the air you need to keep breathing. God keeps our hearts pumping, so the blood does not clot. God loves you more than you will ever know. God protects you daily and does not allow the enemy to steal your life.

God's Word is the most important lesson in life. It equips us with wisdom, revelation, insight, discernment, and understanding. Divine health, prosperity, and soundness of mind are the only treasures that can be transported in the hearts of humanity—and no one can take them from you. It is simple to execute. Just open your mouth, mix it with faith, and believe. You will receive it when you pray it. Know that it's done when you speak His Word with authority. You have been given authority. Jesus's work on the cross commanded this authority, and we must act like it's so. With diligent focus and study, we realize there's much more than what is before us. That empowers us to seek out His truth and change the world around us, the lives of others, and the people we thought we were. You're only sturdy if you study.

The Word of the Master structures the blueprint for life and shows us how to have abundance during the walk. Life is a treasure, and there is a bounteous supply of spiritual gems within us for use on this side of eternity. It's up to the created being to tap into the stored riches accumulated in our spirit man. It is waiting to become a prized possession for you.

CHAPTER 10

Nakedness

It wasn't until the savory taste of the forbidden fruit that Adam and Eve knew they were naked. It was sweet to the flesh but pungent to the spirit. Nakedness prior to the fall of grace was a sense of freedom with nothing to hide, nothing to cover, and no secrets. What is seen is exactly what is being portrayed: no hiding behind an ego, an imperfection, a reputation, a flaw, a fault, a blemish, or a limitation. Just be free and exposed. Nakedness allows you to be seen for who you are with no pretense. Nothing is left to the imagination.

In the computer world, a default is a preselected choice originating in the mind of the computer programmer to specify what something should be. However, the choice has to be adjusted if it does not meet specific criteria. That's what it's like when we are clothed. There is a preconceived idea of what we want others to believe or think concerning who we appear to be. The outward appearance is immaculate and pressed with smoothness to help format opinions. If we only can see beneath the garment of who we really are and what life has dealt us—our integrity and character when no one's looking—would true freedom reign?

A false sense of self will continually make concession decorative of life's pattern trying to vicariously live through what others think. I'm sure that Adam and Eve walked daily in the garden without ever thinking they should be covered. The beauty of the created being was a delight to look upon. After all, God looked and said, "Very good." Adam's response when he first gazed upon the woman was sensational. She was attractive, gorgeous, and stunning. He had seen nothing like her before. Wow was in likelihood his emotion when God brought her to him. What a gift! Perhaps he thought, *What did I do to deserve this? Yes, God, really does love and care about me.* In my opinion, God saved the best for last: the woman.

Without her, procreation could not have happened. She was God's precious gift to man. By exposing her nakedness to him, he would never need anything else besides God to fulfill his need. Imagine never having to be concerned about what to wear, what colors blend together, or what shoes look better. Just wake up and shower in the rich water of the Eden River, breakfast from the tree of life, and walking through paradise—naked and not ashamed, nothing hidden and everything revealed.

Spiritually, our nakedness reveals who we are. Are we able to truthfully honor someone with no hidden agenda and nothing to gain? Can we offer recognition to those who we might differ with in opinion? Can we find glory in someone else's joy and esteem them above ourselves? Do you trust enough to be vulnerable—or are you on the attack?

We tend to hide things from one another in relationships; even those who are married shun the beauty of trusting. Nakedness brings about a peaceful, intimate atmosphere where trust can be exchanged. When we can be trusted, truth is revealed. Living in the true reality of our existence at all times without creating an imposter is pretentious. Nakedness is not just taking off your clothes; it is revealing what's true about you. Nakedness is the actual fact about who we are on the inside of the bodies we house. It's the ultimate expression of how we believe and think. It is the genuine aspect of our character and the integrity of our being.

When we are uncovered, it helps other people know exactly who we are. Being authentic and sincere will take us further in purpose than when we cover our faults, flaws, and imperfections. We are responsible for the deeds done on earth, and we must give an account to God. He is keeping an accurate record of that which is done. We all have a chart in the files of heaven, and recordings are added daily.

Our files disclose how we treat one another, if we are honest and open about concerns that are not always pleasant, and if we are, are we able to speak with kindness and offer resolve rather than criticism.

> Brethren, if a man be overtaken in a fault, ye which are spiritual, restore such a one in the spirit of meekness; considering yourself, lest you be also tempted. (Galatians 6:1 KJV)

The only way to do this is to be spiritual and operate with the Spirit of God abiding inside. We have no judgment. Who knows when we will need restoration? Life is amazing when we simply follow the instruction of His Word.

Nakedness is symbolic of authenticity. It is allowing someone into your world, wanting nothing in return, and being confident about your call in life. There is nothing hidden on the timetable of life that will damage or disrupt another's life. Be ready to present the person who you were created to be—and not whoever you have chosen to be, based on downplaying selfishness.

Strive to become that person if you are not there by spending time in His presence and getting to know the voice of God. He has called you with purpose. Do not allow anyone to define you based on how you appear to them. Your inscription—engraved by God—outweighs the thoughts and assessments of others. God has fine-tuned his design and stamped "fearfully and wonderfully made" on you. We know that His "works are marvelous" and that "my soul knows right well" (Psalm 139:14 KJV). Knowing the truth in reference to what is written in the scriptures makes all the difference for what's truth for me.

> We are having the same spirit of faith, according as it is written, I believe, and therefore have I spoken; we also believe, and therefore speak. (2 Corinthians 4:13 KJV).

Speaking the Word of God is so important to the well-being of our spirits. It is a practice of who we are in Him and deliberately aligning our heads with our hearts. Only saying what God says about us will form the manifestation of His will in you.

In the soulish realm, our minds struggle in conflict with truth. Allowing what's going on around us to dictate who we are or how to think hinders our spiritual growth. We need to be reminded of what God said about who we are. When Eve was brought to Adam, it was like the unveiling of an artist's sculpture. She was a masterpiece created by the Master!

As we yield ourselves to the Lord, we see ourselves as we are. To stand naked before Him speaks volumes. We are not trying to conceal the struggles of life. You cannot conceal anything from Him, and you're only deceiving yourself if you think you can. He knows everything there is to know about us. He knows things about us that we have no clue about.

Positioned in a place of nakedness before God, we say, "Here I am, Lord—flaws and all." We are coming clean in faith, and He will cleanse us through and through. One lovely attribute of our Father is that He only see the woman or man He made us to be. Our repentance and heartfelt sincerity of coming to Him helps lighten the load for what we know was not right in His sight. Our prayer should always be: "Lord, keep me naked before Thee." Never cover yourself with fig leaves to conceal from others what cannot be hidden from God.

Get to Know Him

Jesus spoke in parables to help those in attendance understand his message. He often used earthly stories with heavenly meanings. He used illustrations that people could relate to and connect with where he was taking them spiritually. Relationships are very important in the kingdom of God. For a relationship to develop, those involved must agree and work together to establish the fellowship.

When someone adds chemistry to your life, you hope something will cause you to gain better understanding. You will literally rearrange your schedule to fit their schedule and be with them. If your schedule is filled, you might cancel something to provide time to meet with this person. Emotions and feelings that have been dormant for too long are aroused with the desire to know what has awakened your interest.

Without hesitation, we make known our intent to establish a relationship. There are things we plan and do to make our desires a reality. We make calls, set dinner dates, and explore their interests. There are questions, questions, and more questions. As time passes, we have more information about their likes and dislikes and their character. If they are trustworthy and dependable, we ask about their dreams and visions. We get a feel of their lifestyle, where they are headed in life, and who's going with them. In the times we live in, it does not hurt to do a background check.

To obtain information on what a person is like in character and behavior, there must be quality time spent in their presence. Certain behaviors will be indelibly imprinted upon their hearts and minds. There will be moments in life that are simply unforgettable, and we find ourselves treasuring them forever.

The same process can and should be done on a spiritual plain. Once we except Jesus as Lord of our lives, Savior of our souls, and Keeper of our houses, we must initiate a time for fellowship with Him. We were created for the sole purpose of being with Him throughout eternity. We plan dinner with our significant other, now schedule dinner with God. We break bread; Jesus is the bread of life. The scriptures are the spiritual nourishment that our spirits crave. Feasting on the scriptures will enable you to be endowed with power and the ability to confront whatever the enemy has planned to trip you up with or plan for your demise.

Spending time with God in praise, worship, prayer, fasting, study, solitude, meditation on the Word of God, waiting in His presence, and seeking His face harvest supernatural growth of your spirit man. The same principle applies to your spiritual relationship with Father God. You will come to know Him in ways you have never dreamed of.

When we choose to be seekers with diligence and not just going about it with an attitude of engaging in a casual encounter, we can speak to the mountain—and it is removed. These are the times when God reveals His covenants to you and allows you into the secret place where He resides. By going behind the veil and into the holy of holies, you meet with the Creator of all. Many believers desire to know Him in such intimacy, yet they fail to put forth any effort in doing what it takes to partake of such an awesome place in the Spirit.

People do not arrive with desire alone; there is more. Make good use of the time you have to seek His presence. Follow through on decisions you have made. Never allow barriers to obstruct your vision. Determine godly principles. Commit to living by them no matter what. Being steadfast and unmovable when challenge occurs will land you on the solid ground. The scripture says, "And having done all, to stand. (Ephesians 6:13 KJV) When the storms of life hit, and it appears to be dark—and you think God is not around—He's right there in the background, working it out for your good.

Worship is the most intimate discipline in the kingdom. Worship will take you places you have not been if you remain there long enough to part the heavens and usher in the presence of His Spirit. Create an environment that is conducive to the moving of His Spirit. God loves to be praised. He loves to be worshipped. He seeks out those who will worship Him. Would you like to be sought after by God? If your response is yes, then it behooves you to spend your time worshipping Him.

Scheduling time with Him each day to meet in awe of His presence and hearing a word from heaven will enrich the soul and give spiritual momentum. Desire a robust spirit. In the natural world, some of us love to eat. We are physically robust, and we can take that same energy and apply it to our spirit man. Our heavenly Father knows all—and who better to plan and guide your day? He will give you inside information on what is happening and show you things to come.

An exchange takes place in His holy presence. Thanksgiving and praise ignite a spiritual flaming process that cleanses the soul and revives the spirit with enrichment to full spiritual potential, which enables us to operate in the power of God. God will reveal Himself to whomever is willing to spend time with Him. In a marriage, the two become one. God wants us to be one with Him. No hidden plans—everything open.

When our hands are lifted in adoration to Him, and we begin to tell Him how awesome He is, how much we love and desire Him for no other reason than who He is, it affirms an avowal of who we are committed to. Some believers come to worship services faithfully and believe this is all that is necessary. They think it does not take that much to know Him. It takes that and more. He is "seeking such to worship him" (John 4:23 KJV).

When we emerge with intense worship, the expectation is that He is present to heal, deliver, and set the captive free. When we saturate ourselves in the presence, His ability becomes our capability. We operate with great exploits. Seeking the Father has to be done on purpose and not haphazardly. The way has been made through the work of Christ on the cross, and the renting of the veil torn in pieces from top to bottom provided a place for you at His throne. I ask the same question the eunuch asked Phillip in the book of Acts: "What doeth hinder thee?" (Acts 8:36 KJV).

Prayer

Prayer is such a powerful spiritual discipline to develop. We all can access the heavens and cause things, situations, circumstances, and people to change. If we believe when praying and allow faith to mix with scripture, many would see prayer as necessary and not optional:

> If my people which are called by my name shall humble themselves, and pray, and seek my face, and turn from their wicked ways; then will I hear from heaven, and will forgive their sin, and heal the land. (2 Chronicles 7:14 KJV)

There is a magnitude of blessing in this scripture: humility, forgiveness, healing, prayer, a turn from wickedness, and seeking God. Prayer is simply doing business with God. He wants to do the things He says in this verse, and it is up to you to meet the requirement that releases Him to flow in your life.

Every promise of God has principles that coordinate with receiving the blessing. We have a part to do. It is best to cooperate with God. The Bible lets us know that we are workers together with Him (2 Corinthians 6:1 KJV). It does not say "workers for Him." It says *with* Him. This allows us to avoid getting ahead of God and doing it our way. Prayer brings you into the supernatural power of exchange: His super on our natural. How explosive is that? How did Samson kill a lion with his bare hand, catch three hundred foxes and set their tails on fire, and then slay the Philistines while being blind? God's supernatural power came upon a natural man, which increased his ability to overpower the circumstance. Beloved, God has not changed. Jesus Christ is the same yesterday, today, and forever (Hebrews 13:8 KJV).

Utilize the acronym PUSH (pray until something happens). Prayer should be second nature in our lives and not a "when all else fails, we pray." God is a "right now" God. He never sleeps or slumbers. He knows when a bird falls from a tree. Jesus spent so much time in prayer and seeking the Father. Jesus, the Son of God, could have called legions of angelic beings, and they would have responded to his call. Instead, He prayed to the Father to move on His behalf.

When Jesus prayed, the Bible says, "He looked up to heaven" (Mark 6:41 KJV). He rose early in the morning to pray. He spent all night praying. He taught his disciples to pray. He taught us how to pray. Jesus did nothing without praying first. The most powerful and effective prayer is praying the Word of God. If we say what God has said, then God have to do what we have said. It is His word, and "it shall never return unto Him void" (Isaiah 55:11 KJV).

CHAPTER 11

A Flash from the Past

Seven years after graduating from high school, I knew it was time to make decisions that would help guide me into my future. I did not want to be traveling through life, barely making ends meet. I witnessed classmates going off to college, getting their degrees, and returning home to proud parents. The one thing I wanted in life was to make sure that my parents were delighted in the way their raising me turned out. I had a mother who worked hard at living a decent life in front of her children. She maintained excellent work habits once she accepted a job when we were much older and could take care of ourselves.

Her example in our home surely was honored and mimicked in my life and that of my sisters as well. Both parents instilled good principles along with life lessons as we matured in age. The adage that says, "What a child lives is what the child will learn," is true. There were things that my parents just did not do in the home. I never recall seeing liquor being brought into our home. There was not a wine cellar or a wineglass in the house. So, drinking was not a temptation for me or my sisters. My dad would take a drink only on the weekends outside of our home with his friends. Never would he bring any in the house.

My mom sat with me during the interview with Weaver Airlines to plan a career as a flight attendant. She allowed me to attend modeling school and take administrative classes in a program at the school of business. I never did seek employment in either of those, but I was able to incorporate what I learned into certain areas of my life. Even though I did well in the classes and graduated from the programs, there was never any passion within to pursue a lifelong obligation.

There have to be a driving force within that creates a hunger to thrive in the area in which you're supposed to function. During the time I enrolled in each program, there was excitement about fulfilling the desired goals and great expectation about being able to help others along the way. I learned to write shorthand and increased my speed to 120 words per minute. As I envisioned working in the corporate world with executives at large companies with perks and great benefits, the dream just did not feel good in my spirit.

Learning how to model in a program that I took with a childhood friend seemed very rewarding and glamorous. We learned how to walk with grace and poise, sit and enter a vehicle, put on makeup like the professionals in Hollywood, coordinate colors, and put an outfit together in minutes. We were taught to wear our clothing with taste and elegance. I mastered the pivots and turns and the walk down the runway. We were waiting for our time in the big city of New York, with the lights, cameras, agents, magazine covers, and everything that comes along with a career in the industry.

Yes, it was a wonderful program, and we learned so much about how to conduct ourselves in this arena. In fast-paced fashion shows, we were changing outfits for the catwalk. It was truly a preparation for the opportunity I had the honor of participating with real professional models in California. I had my makeup done, my hair styled, and help with dressing. We were modeling apparel from high-end merchants, boutiques, and department stores. It was great because my younger sister was there to witness it all. She has always been my best friend and always supported me in my endeavors.

What an exciting time—and it was even more of a thrill to be chosen to do that job. A manager at the hospital wanted someone to represent the department, and I was picked. It was beyond me how it happened, but I attributed it to God working in my behalf. We had to go through a process of practicing the walk and changing clothes. It was all timed. We met with the coordinator of the stores to choose the clothing to model. It was a huge project in the community.

Dignitaries and corporate CEOs raised funds for the hospital with a fashion show, a fancy dinner, and a silent auction.

I was in three or four scenes, and knowing the industry was certainly an advantage. On the runway, they allowed me to model my own boots with an outfit. It was truly invigorating to hear the cheers from the tables: "Strut, sister," "Go Loretta," "That's right," and "Go, girl." There were so many encouraging comments being made on my behalf. The professionals had height that was beyond me. It was not what I was called to do. In the moment, it was extremely beautiful, but something on the inside—that quiet, still inner feeling of peace—has always led me in the right direction.

Missing Identity

The static condition of positively identifying who I am was not yet a reality. After educating myself in what I thought I wanted to do, I remained in a state of confusion. I was just not feeling it. Initially, I was so caught up in the hype of being a flight attendant, a model, or an administrative assistant that I forgot to search my spirit man to see if it was a notion of God. I was unaware of the who, why, and how of my life, but I knew that something had to be done. Life is short—and wasting years without purpose is more devastating than death. Living among those in life, walking as though you are dead, and making no contributions toward leaving a legacy is tragic.

There are times when we think we know who we are. When the question is asked of us, our answer is the name we were given by our parents. I am not convinced that is who we are. It is simply what we prefer to be called when we are acknowledged or approached by someone. Our names are important, and I have learned that it's tied to our purpose. We should always be informed about the meaning of how it can guide us to our destinies. For some of us, God's guidance is evident when our parents named us. At other times, when we're asked who we are, a common response is what we do rather than who we are: I'm a doctor, I'm a police officer, I'm a nurse, or I'm a CEO. It's sad when people are not spiritually sound about who they are.

The children of Israel wandered in the wilderness for forty years. These were people who God loved, provided for, and guided on their path. Prior to the wilderness expedition, they were slaves under the leadership of Pharaoh. He did not heed the voice of God. Throughout their captivity of more than four hundred years, the Israelites were covered by the grace of God. Their protection was not of the natural realm; it was of the supernatural realm. God had devised a plan for their rescue with the birth of Moses, and in His own timing, the deliverance was inevitable.

Was it chance for Moses to be found by the pharaoh's daughter and then be raised by his own mother? Was this coincidence? Not at all. This was a divinely orchestrated strategy of God to usher in His plan for their departure from captivity. After he was nursed of his natural mother, "She brought him to Pharaoh's daughter" (Exodus 2:10 KJV). He was given the name "Moses." As the chosen one, he was groomed and prepped by the dynasty of Egypt. Not fully aware of his mission to lead them out of Egypt, he was exiled. God's plan for him was on hold.

There are times in our lives when we hinder the plans of God because of sheer disobedience, true ignorance, or outright rebellion. Moses was a few lengths ahead of God in defending the Hebrews and bringing the Egyptian to his demise. When we feel like we have an unction of what we think God wants to do in us, we are prompted to move quickly. If we do this without praying and seeking God, we get off track. It happened to Abraham, Sarah, Joseph, and Jonah to name a few. It also occurs in our lives if we are honest enough to admit our shortcomings. God's desire is that every one of His created beings comes to know His plan for them and in what season it will manifest.

My plans of being a flight attendant, a model, or an administrative assistant were never the plans God had for me. Though I was firmly set on accomplishing these three disciplines, giving serious time and attention to achieving the goals, it was all in opposition to what the Master of my soul attached to my life's resume.

The wonderful blessing I learned was that He did not give up on me and throw in the towel. God gives us second, third, fourth, and fifth chances if needed. God will be there to reel you back to the place He needs you to be. I never received a dishonorable discharge from Him. I was still needed in His kingdom. In this world, you can be treated unfairly and ostracized when you do what's right and stand up for your God-given rights and privileges.

God will clue you in to who you really are. We are God's craftmanship, made in His image and likeness, and our identities are in Him. He will guide us through every path in life, but it is up to us to heed the call and say yes to the course. God's directions are not mere suggestions that we are to take lightly. It is His intention that we're to experience heaven on earth when we are in alignment with His Word.

> Everything we could ever need for life and godliness has already been deposited in us by his divine power. For all this was lavished upon us through the rich experience of knowing him who has called us by name and invited us to come to him through a glorious manifestation of his goodness. (2 Peter 1:3 TPT)

It is written that we've been given "all things that pertain to life." What's left out of all? He has given us the entire totality of everything. Nothing that relates to liveliness and sanctity is withheld. Unless we discover what the treasures are, we'll never know what exactly belongs to us. These blessings and promises are obtained through the knowledge of Him. This is vital to learning who we are in Christ.

The time spent in God's Word shapes our spirits to lean more toward His desired plan. I was given clear direction and was certain that it was God, but for some odd reason, I failed to take it further through prayer. I would have found the next step. The Holy Spirit will set off an alarm, and there is no doubt that we have missed it.

Abraham, Moses, Jonah, and several others missed the mark. They went through trying times and situations that were not written in their scripts. They delayed the plan of God for their lives. It is not always how we begin; the important part is how we end. How does the story end? All three men had overwhelming encounters that caused havoc in their lives, but God intervened and caused them to accomplish their God-given assignments.

God's will shall be done in heaven and on earth. Abraham's home life was wrecked when he yielded to his wife's bright idea, but twenty-five years later, God's plan for Isaac, the son of promise, came to pass. Moses's hot temper cost him forty years in the desert before he could carry out the plan for the deliverance of Israel, but he did it. He never fulfilled the second half of his destiny in making it into the promised land that flowed with milk and honey. His disobedience prevented him from entering.

When God gives instruction to speak, and you strike, there can be consequences that are costly. Jonah was in the belly of a great fish for three days. I can only imagine the horror of feeling trapped somewhere and thinking that no one will ever find me. All he had to do was do what God instructed. He eventually fulfilled God's plan to minister prophetically to Nineveh.

Along the journey, there will be times of distraction and influence from others. They will try to deter our walk of purpose and postpone God's plan because we are wandering in the wilderness of life and trying to figure out who we are. It's given from the beginning of time, if we wholeheartedly search and seek out the One who caused it to be. We are not held accountable during the initial training of our formative years, yet once we are mature enough to know right from wrong, we are. No matter where we find ourselves on the plane in life, our heavenly Father desires us to know Him.

The Sovereign One is the only One who has written our story. God's signature is on the inscription of who we really are. His logo should be centered in our lives. We should be letting the world see who we are—and whose we are. Let's reveal our true identities. Let's walk in the definite purpose that was ordained for us. Let's execute with intention to be the people we really are by going forth and doing great things in the kingdom of God.

> The entire universe is standing on tiptoe, yearning to see the unveiling of God's glorious sons and daughters! (Romans 8:19 TPT)
>
> For [even the whole] creation [all nature] waits eagerly for the children of God to be revealed. (Romans 8:19 AMP)

Let's be among those who will unveil and reveal to this world God's great and mighty men and women of faith who are "not ashamed of the Gospel of Christ, because it is the power of God unto salvation to everyone who believes" (Romans 1:16 KJV).

We are the answer to this world's issues. We are filled with the power of heaven to operate in this earth just as God does in heaven:

> After this manner therefore pray ye, Our Father which are in heaven, Hollowed be thy name. Thy kingdom come. Thy will be done in earth as it is in heaven. (Matthew 6:9 KJV)

The Lord's Prayer qualifies us to do the same as God does in the heavens by taking our rightful place here on this earth by knowing who we are in Him.

The results of His will being done on this planet comes from the faithful and willing believers who respond to His call. Taking heed of the assignment from heaven requires being sincere and serious about what has been released to our stewardship.

So, who do you think you are?

CHAPTER 12

She's God's Woman

Inkster, Michigan, had a population of approximately thirty-nine thousand in the 1960s. There were people who were gifted, talented, and witty. Inkster, about twenty-seven miles west of Detroit, was known for having the most beautiful girls and well-dressed guys. There were several elementary schools, but only one junior high and high school. Back then, parents did not play when it came to education and well-being.

Education was priority, and you had to study and learn how to adapt in a world that refused to address you as human and respect your character. some people would ignore the brilliance God gave you. I remember every one of my schoolteachers and how passionate they were when it came to our learning. These teachers went above and beyond the call of duty to help us succeed in life. They were well educated and wanted to produce well-educated students to pass on prosperous lives to those who would come after us. One teacher would say, "I have my education—and you have to get yours."

In those days, there was not as much distraction and rebellion as we see in today's world. We could pray and state the Pledge of Allegiance, which kept us respecting the gift that God placed there for our growth.

So much was going on in America, the nation that was known around the world as the "greatest country." I imagine for some it was, and for others, it was not. People were fighting for civil rights, voting rights, jobs, and housing rights—in addition to simply making a living to care for their families. Times were hard. My parents did the best they could with the cards they were dealt, and my heart was glad. No matter how bad things were, they always included family time, lived a respectful life in front of us, and taught us morals and values. I owe it to the wonderful mom and dad who God entrusted with our lives.

In 1969, I finished eighth grade at Fellrath Junior High School. High school was the next exciting phase in life. Everyone pretty much knew each other, and it was a great time in life. Motown was the music of the day, and the entertainers were in our reach. The Marvelettes, our hometown girls, were recording number one hit records. The Supremes and Temptations along with a host of others from Detroit's music scene were topping the charts with their latest recordings.

During those times, Detroit was the place to be. Roller skating originated there, and it is the capital of the world when it comes to roller skating. Detroit has a style of its own; no one can do it like the Motor City. The big three automakers were producing the latest vehicles, which helped keep the city strong and vibrant. For music and cars, you had to come through Detroit. What a blessing it was to have such great gifts, talents, and love flowing throughout a region.

In September, it was time to return to school. High School required a sense of maturity, and vision was a much broader aspect than before. Upon registering for classes, I noticed that I was placed in the college prep class. The students who had achieved higher academic grades were placed as a group to study together for the next four years: foreign language, science, math, history, music, art, English, and government.

There are times when God has placed something on the inside of you that you are not aware of, and that very thing hasn't been nurtured or sought out. There are times when you've been called upon and respected as one of the class elite, but you never believed you have been blessed to receive such favor. In French class, I was not giving it my all. I learned a few phrases and could speak it, but the translation of what I was saying was not always clear. Our teacher was frustrated with me and passed me over when he went around the room to have the students speak. I felt embarrassed and sad because I had done it to myself by not studying as I should have.

After two years of six hours a day, five days a week, with the same classmates, I no longer wanted to be a part of the group. I asked to be taken out and placed with the other students. What a mistake! I no longer focused on studying and planning my future. I wanted to be with the "regular" students and not the brainiacs—even though I was considered one too. She had no understanding of who she was.

There were times that I would not go to class, especially physical education. We had to swim, and my hair would be wet, curl up so tight, and be unmanageable. No way was I doing my hair two or three times a week, and Momma had no extra money for the hairdresser. I would pass all the classes I attended without issue; it was the ones I did not care for that I had to make up in order to graduate on time. By the time I reached eleventh grade and began to think about college and what to do in life, my GPA was not what it should have been. That was a wake-up call!

We met with the academic counselor and got recommendations for further educational plans. After checking my transcripts and the classes I need to complete for graduation my counselor said, "There is not one college that will accept you with grades like this."

If I planned to graduate on time with my class, I would have to take night classes to make up. Reality set in, and I did what was required to make it happen. I could not disappoint my parents. They always thought I was on top of things when it came to school.

When I walked across that stage and received my diploma, Momma was looking on and smiling. My academic counselor's words would ring loud in my ears for years to come. I would never pursue college because I believed no college would accept me for higher education. I had a desire to be a flight attendant and applied to Weaver Airlines right after high school. I was accepted, and the school sent a representative to my home to interview me. My mother sat with me during the interview, and everything worked out to take a correspondent course and make payments.

After the theory portion was done, I would be flown to their headquarters for training. We agreed that I would train to be a flight attendant, but after about six months, I found out that there was a breach of contract. I was given another curriculum to study. This was disappointing, and the words of my counselor kept me from applying to a college or university. Words have power, and what we do with them determines how we function in life. We either receive them or reject them.

My grades were not what they should have been, and I forgot what I was capable of doing. When I got back on track to graduate on time from high school, I was accepted at Weaver Airlines. Once I was born again, what could possibly be withheld from me? That's the question I had to asked myself. With my knowledge of God and who He is, it was time for production of His Word. I had learned how He saw me. He created me with wisdom and understanding that I am able to do all things through Him.

I no longer rely on my own way of thinking. I have been gifted with a renewed mind. My old life has been replaced with a new set of spiritual standards that qualify me to enter and operate on a higher level. During my revelation, I began to understand that the powers of heaven have truly been given to us. The statement that Jesus spoke to Martha at the grave of Lazarus changed my entire perspective about who I'm supposed to be. It was time to walk in it!

I would no longer be hindered by the lies of the devil. I would no longer think that I was incapable of carrying out the Lord's will in this earthly realm. I would no longer allow fear, doubt, or disbelief to be a part of my life. It was time to take a stand and engage in that which I believed to be true. Jesus said that "signs would follow those that believe" (Mark 16:17 KJV), and I considered myself a believer. It was up to me to act upon it, and it was up to Him to bring it to pass.

Casting out the fear and distractions that disconnected me from my God-guided life had an impact on my contribution to the kingdom:

> But ye shall receive power, after the Holy Ghost has come upon you: and ye shall be witnesses unto me both in all Jerusalem, and in all Judaea, and in Samaria, and to the most uttermost part of the earth. (Acts 1:8 KJV)

The word *power* in Greek is *dynamis*, which indicates strength, power, and ability. The power of God breeds miracles. I experienced the power of God manifesting in what I was led to do.

Gifts of Healing and the Working of Miracles

I realized that God's power is just as real as the legs I use to walk. There was a power failure in Broken Arrow, Oklahoma, and my two sons were there with me. Ever-Increasing Faith Ministries is one of my favorites to listen to. It was said the power outage would last for quite some time. I had so much hunger to be fed the Word of God through this ministry that I told my children it wasn't right that I had to miss it because of an outage. I took authority over that situation, and when I commanded the power to come back into that apartment, it happened immediately. The power was restored, and the children were amazed at what they had experienced.

That was just a taste of what God wanted to show me through His mighty power. That gave me ammunition to fire with faith for other things. As God began to show Himself to me through various situations—which I knew no one else except Him could have done—my plan was set. I said. "God, there is nothing I can't believe you for." After the powerful presence of God filled my bedroom in Broken Arrow, the miracles began.

For the baby with the hole in his heart and Down syndrome, God supernaturally caused tissue to grow over the hole. The professor with the bladder cancer healed. The young woman with sickle cell became free of pain after strong narcotics couldn't relieve her pain. The two barren young ladies who could not conceive but gave birth within a year of being prayed over. One tried to get pregnant for thirteen years and could not until the Holy Spirit came upon her in one of the pre-op rooms at work. God can move wherever He chooses to.

After my mother's stroke, God allowed me to pray over her in the emergency room—and she left the hospital in three days with no neurological deficits. A man died in the operating room, and the team worked on this code for forty-five minutes. God led me to go in there to pray against all odds and bring him back to life. The doctor screamed and declared, "It's a miracle!"

I swatted a firefly by mistake, and it fell to the ground. I prayed to God and apologized that I did not mean to do that. He touched the bug and raised it up. I moved my hand as close as I could three times and believed God all along. Within twenty minutes, that firefly rose up and flew away. My friend watched me pray for the bug and talk to it. She was just undone when the firefly lit up and flew away.

A young child on a plane was crying uncontrollably, and the mother and flight attendant could not comfort her. The flight attendant and I thought it was the pressure mounting in her ears. The Holy Spirit told me to ask the mother if I could pray for the baby. I did, and the mom gave me permission to pray. As I began to pray, I mentioned to the mom that I needed to touch the baby's ears. She agreed. I held her head between my hands and covered her ears. Within seconds, she stopped crying and fell asleep. I held her head during the entire flight, and the mother was astonished.

I explained that God was touching her child and that God did it for her to believe, increase her faith in Him, and share her story of what He did for them. The baby remained asleep with her head between my hands until the final descent. Just before landing, she opened her eyes and awakened with the peace of God and no irritation.

On my next flight, a couple was across the aisle from me. The husband had a consistent cough, and I began to pray and ask God to cover me and not allow any germs to come in contact with me. I didn't want to get sick.

While praying for myself, God changed the prayer to benefit the gentleman. God said, "You should be praying for him not to cough—he needs the healing." I agreed with Him and began to pray that God would touch his body and silence his coughing. God is so faithful, and He did just what He asked me to pray. That is why prayer is so important. God can't move until someone asks Him to. Throughout the entire flight, the man never coughed again. I sat in amazement at the power of my Daddy.

During the descent, God told me to ask the man if he noticed that he was no longer coughing during the flight. I had to let him know that prayer was prayed for him—and that God had touched his body. I told the Lord that I would say it when we landed. That's not what He wanted. God insisted that I do it during the descent. Fear gripped me, and I had to overcome the evil spirit to be free to say it.

I finally came to grips with being bold, and I had a conversation with the woman who I assumed was his wife. I asked if the man next to her was her husband, and she replied, "Yes." I told her what God had said for me to say, and she relayed it to her husband on the other side of her. He said, "Yes, I notice that I have not coughed in a while. Thank you for praying for me." He told me about his knee problems and asked me to pray for that. It truly was a witness that God is real, and they could have been ripe for gathering into the kingdom of God. Only God knows.

A middle-aged lady came to church with a cane, a nasal cannula, and an oxygen tank. She came to the altar during the ministering of salvation and gave her life back to the Lord. We took those at the altar to the prayer room for further ministering to those who need prayers. As I was praying for a woman who was dealing with emotional pain and conflict, I looked at the woman with the nasal cannula and oxygen tank. I stopped and asked if she wanted to be healed.

"Yes."

I said, "If you are serious and can believe God can heal you, it's going to happen."

She said, "I do believe that."

I told her to finish writing her information on the card and allow me to finish ministering to the woman I was with. After I completed the ministry, I walked over to the lady and spoke God's Word over her.

She explained that she had a collapsed lung.

I said, "God created that lung, and He can inflate it back to its original state. Do you believe that?"

"Yeah."

I prayed over her, and I sensed that the Holy Spirit was all over her, doing the work He sent me to minister. I said, "No matter what it looks like right now, God has healed your body."

She agreed.

The next Sunday, someone entered the church and stopped to talk to the greeter.

The greeter pointed to the area where I was standing. I had no idea it was the lady I had prayed over. As she made her way over to where I was standing, I noticed she had no cane, cannula, or oxygen tank. She was running over to show me what God had done in her body.

I said, "He's God!"

She gave her testimony to the entire church that Sunday because the pastor wanted her story told. They saw her come in one way and come back another way.

I visited a church that I wanted to join. It was a Sunday, and I arrived a little later than planned. As I entered the sanctuary, I was seated near the back on the right-hand side. The usher sat me right next to a blind Caucasian man. I knew he was blind because he had a probing cane.

At a certain point in the service, the pastor instructed everyone to pray for the person next to them as the Lord led us. As I began to pray, I put my left hand on the man's right leg to pray for him. I knew that God was working on his behalf. It is an awesome experience when I can sense an active anointing present. God begins to move, and special faith is at work. I believe when I pray because that is the Word:

> Therefore, I say unto you, what things so ever you desire, when you pray, believe that you receive them, and ye shall have them. (Mark 11:24 KJV)

Believing is an act of faith that seem almost tangible. It is the substance of the thing you're hoping for. The next Sunday, the man came to church seeing. The pastor of that church still tells the story to this day. God is amazing.

There are times when I hear the Spirit of God speaking to my spirit, and I know when to move out in faith. There are other times when the center of my left hand feels hot. This is another supernatural indicator of God wanting to heal someone nearby.

My sister in the Lord and I were eating lunch at a Mexican restaurant after the worship service, and I began experiencing warmth in my left hand. I said, "God wants to heal someone, but I do not know who it is." If the heat intensifies when I extend my hand toward them, I move closer to them.

It was a challenge to decipher. I stretched out my arm to the left, and I felt an increase in heat. When I stretched it out to the table behind me, there was another increase in heat. I said, "I'm not sure which one God wants to heal."

She asked if I wanted her to get their attention by staring at them.

I was truly at the mercy of the Lord in making the decision. I said, "I think it's the one on my left."

Before long, the gentleman at the table went to the rest room.

I asked the woman if he was her husband, and he was. I shared everything that God had said, and she said, "How do you know that?"

I told her that I knew nothing except for what God spoke to me concerning him. I was led to share a few scriptures that confirmed what had happened, and the scripture commanded the Lord's power. When the husband returned to the table, his wife asked me to share what I had said.

He was startled and said, "How do you know this?"

I helped them understand that God is real and that He loves them and wants to heal his body. Right then and there, he willfully wanted prayer. We prayed immediately at their table, and God did what He always does when we are obedient and trust Him to do His work.

At Sunday morning worship, I love to worship God. The praise and worship were true, and the gifts were focused upon the Lord. His presence filled the room, and my hands felt warm. I said, "God, what is going on? I've never had this happen before where both hands are heated." As the worship was happening, I could feel the heat increasing in my palms.

"God, what am I supposed to do? Who needs healing?" I checked my surroundings, saw a boy with bilateral hearing aids, and understood why my hands were hot.

I asked the woman who had brought him to service if I could pray for him because God wanted to heal him. She gave me the go-ahead, and I positioned his head between my hands and began to pray. When I sense a tangible anointing present, I pray until I get a release from God to know that His work has been completed. I hadn't noticed one of the ushers watching it all and taking pictures with his phone. Once God finished, I was finished. I asked the woman to remove the hearing aid so I could see if he could hear me.

I whispered, "Say Jesus is Lord."

He said, "Jesus is Lord."

I asked him to say Praise the Lord, and he said, "Praise the Lord."

I asked her to remove the other hearing aid and began speaking to him—and he was able to hear and repeat everything I said.

She was radiating with joy as he repeated the words. She told me that I needed to let the pastor know what had happened.

I said, "No, you have to inform the pastor because it's your testimony—not mine."

She got the attention of the pastor during the greeting portion of the service and shared the greatness of God with him.

Afterward, the pastor asked me to come up front with the child and explain what had happened with the boy's hearing.

I told how I was led to him and how God healed him. I showed the congregation his hearing aids and whispered in his ear, and he repeated every word I said. When I asked if he wanted his hearing aids back, he said, "No! I will never have to wear them again because I can hear."

> Oh, that men would praise the Lord for His goodness,
> and for His wonderful works to the children of men.
> (Psalm 107:8 KJV)

Believing is Receiving

Time does not allow me to write about every healing and miracle in this book. God's greatness has led us to this point. God healed a woman with breast cancer. A younger woman had colon cancer at age twenty-one. The doctors said she had tumors and scheduled her for surgery. Our prayer team prayed for her the night before her surgery, and she was healed. The doctors could not locate any cancer or tumors in her body.

A prayer request came in from Texas. A rare form of cancer had invaded a woman's body. The doctor's report was grave, and the options were radiation, chemo, and drugs. Fervent prayers went forth in the name of Jesus. I asked her to text me pictures of where the cancer was in her body. I had noticed the areas on her lower extremities when I was there a month before, and I was wondering what was going on. I was led to lay hands on the pictures and pray for a few days.

I was later told that she had recorded the prayer and listened to it over and over again until the Word of God saturated her being. The manifestation of her healing occurred about thirty days later. The doctors decided that there was no need for radiation, chemo, or strong drugs because they could no longer find cancer in her body. The biopsies and other tests came back negative.

During the writing of this chapter, God impressed upon me to pray for a dear person. This coworker was very close to my heart. She had been paralyzed for a number of years after surgery. She has kept a positive attitude and maintained her beautiful smile over the years.

I mentioned that I would come visit, pray, and believe God would touch her body. I have pain cards that have a holistic approach to alleviating pain from the body without drugs or narcotics. It's a blessing from God that was researched and designed by top doctors. It was understood that I would come on Friday, but they also had a couple of friends there to stay overnight. I knew about one of them but not the other. My sump pump was not operating properly, and I had to get someone over to look at it. I let her know that I would be there within a few days.

Distractions can hinder the work being done. In the Gospels, Jesus had to excuse some people from the room when God wanted to work a miracle by raising a maid from death's hold. When He told those in attendance that "she wasn't dead but sleeps, they laughed him to scorn." He removed them from the room. "He went into the room and took her by the hand, and she arose" (Matthew 9:25 KJV).

In the house, there was one believer and one nonbeliever. I don't think it was coincidence that my sump pump stopped working at that time. God's delay is not denial. There has to be an atmosphere where faith is present—and believers are on one accord.

At their home on Monday, the pain was all over her body. The tears were flowing like water from a faucet. I let her know it was about to get better.

She said, "When the weather is cold, my body aches uncontrollably with muscle spasms."

I began to comfort them, pray, and speak God's Word. I explained how the pain cards would stop the pain. "As soon as I get the cards on your body, the pain will be gone in a few minutes."

I knew the cards were the answer to her pain, but I did not know what God was going to do next. I strategically placed six pain cards on her body. I placed two on her upper left arm, two on her lower right arm, one across her right foot, and one on her right leg, just below the knee. I said, "Give it a few minutes—and your pain will be history."

Crying, she mustered a smile and said, "Okay."

An atmosphere had to be created that would usher the presence of God into the room. As I shared the scriptures and testimonies of what God had done in the lives of others, I helped her understand that He is not a respecter of one and not the other.

After about five minutes, she said, "Jazz, I feel a difference in my pain. It's not all gone yet, but it has lightened up. I sure do feel a difference." I knew that her pain would be completely gone in a little while—and it was.

God is faithful and always up to something great. I had no inkling that He was about to work a miracle right before our eyes. She had been a quadriplegic for six years but she began to move her second and third finger on her left hand. The radiance on her face and the excitement in her voice rang out loudly. She says, "Look at my hand. My fingers are moving. I have not been able to move my fingers in six years. Wow!"

I grabbed my phone to make a video. God touched each finger, and they moved. The excitement in the room radiated throughout the house, and she began yelling for her daughters to come see what she was able to do with her hand. It wasn't long before she began to move four fingers, and then she was able to stretch them. "Wow, I have not been able to move my fingers for six years." It was a great time to be present. Her caretaker, her daughters, her daughter's friend, and I witnessed the miraculous event.

God was not just moving her fingers. His powerful anointed presence began to work in her entire hand. She lifted her hand off the pillow, and her fingers began to spread. She hadn't been able to do that for six years. She began to spread her fingers apart, flex her hand forward and backward, and twirl it around and around. Her wrist had not moved in six years. Her arm raised high, and the left arm was moving normally. Everything that happens to us that is good—God does it!

She had been to several doctors, a hand specialist, neurologists, physical therapy, and others, and nothing had ever happened. She praised God and said that if she hadn't been there to see it, she would not have believed it.

I videoed every stage of what God did that day. It is amazing for us to witness the power of God at work, and that's because we often forget who He is. That is what He does—and that's who He is. He's God! Rather than being amazed and shocked at His power in action, we must expect it to happen every time. It's according to your faith!

When all odds are against us, we must kick things into high gear. We must put the pedal to the metal in our faith; faith is the gas that initiates the drive. I inherited a home with an $87,000 mortgage attached to it. My name was on the house, but I was never responsible for the mortgage. When I made inquiry into the matters of this situation, I found out that I was not going to be given any detailed information concerning the loan.

The only response I received from the bank was in the form of a question: "Are you going to make a payment?"

I said, "No, I'm not."

This went on for several months, and I was submissive to everything they asked of me except for making a payment. I sent in notarized copies of the documents required by the bank, but none of it was enough for them. I was at the point of no return.

I received a message that my late husband and I could get the house back for five to eight thousand dollars. When I returned the call, I was given information that I was not aware of. I had no knowledge that the house had been in foreclosure since I had not lived there in ten years. The house would be auctioned off, and we would have the first offer to redeem it. The person on the phone was not aware that my husband was deceased. I thanked her for the information and thought, *It's worth that, and the cost is much less than the mortgage owed.*

They asked me to call two days before the auction to get the starting price.

I agreed to do that. I was given three different dates for the auction over a three-month period. I would call the number two days before, but another date would be set. I called in June, July, and August, and each one was postponed. The last date set was for September.

I said, "God, this is frustrating. Why is it being postponed each time?" I did not hear one word from God, but I said, "You know I trust You."

A few months later, I thought about why the other company wanted me to call them with the starting bid two days early. They would have time to plan their strategy for making a bid on the house. I decided that I would not call them. God is so good. I never had a reason to call them because each date had been postponed.

I had been given the run-a-round for several months. A loan officer wanted to help me, but because my name was not on the loan, her hands were tied. I said, "God, You must move in this situation on Your baby's behalf."

That was exactly what He was doing. I finally got in touch with another department leader who promised to do everything possible to keep me abreast of everything. She kept her word, and things began to move, but she was limited in the information she could disclose to me.

In September, I called to find out the starting bid. I was told that the auction had been canceled. I asked why, but they only directed me to call the bank for further information. My frustration was growing deeper. *They've canceled the entire opportunity to buy the house back at what I considered a great price of five to eight thousand dollars? Oh my God! Now what?*

I spoke with the person who was in charge of my case, but she had no knowledge about why the auction had been canceled—but God did. After the conversation, I was disappointed and aggravated. *Why, God? Why?* I heard nothing from Him.

My mother always said, "Loretta,. no news is good news." It sure was.

After a week or two, I received a letter from the bank that the mortgage for $87,000 had been forgiven. "The debt is canceled. You may continue to live in the house, sell the house, or do whatever you desire. Your debt has been canceled, but it must be reported to the IRS and will be considered income."

God does everything well. The debt was not reported in my name because my name was never on the loan. I also found out that the homeowner's insurance and property taxes had been paid up until July of the following year. You are talking about a party God—and I had a Holy Ghost party when that information came to me.

I call one of my attorneys and read the letter to him. He suggested we meet and look it over. I arrived at the coffee shop first, and he said, "Loretta, you must be living right because this kind of thing don't just happen."

I said, "Yes, I promise I do live right before God. God is faithful to His Word. As He said in Deuteronomy 28:13, 'And the Lord shall make you the head and not the tail; above only and not be beneath; if that thou hearken unto the commandments of the Lord thy God, which I command thee this day, to observe and to do them.' I truly came out on top of this one. Praise God! We all can and should no matter what the circumstances are. He is faithful."

Ecclesiastes encourages us to "hear the conclusion to the whole matter" (Ecclesiastes 12:13 KJV). God's Word is true whether you believe it or not. It does not change. His Word will last forever. Jesus said, "Heaven and earth shall pass away, but my Words shall not pass away" (Matthew 24:35 KJV). It is all according to our faith that we can know and understand who we are in Christ. All the times I've missed God, taking the path I thought was right for me, and all the detours that led to nowhere were part of what kept me from knowing who I am.

I now know that I am God's woman. I am anointed by Him to fulfill that which was prophesied over me years prior to becoming the one He created me to be. It was a long road, and I had to learn how to trust God with everything, know His voice, and learn how to pray effectively. From studying His Word, I knew He would "never leave or forsake me" (Hebrews 13:5 KJV). He would greatly benefit my life. He always helps those in need. Yield yourself to His guidance—and discover who you really are.

Who do you think you are? The answer lies in the One who created you for His glory—and nothing more. Arrive, bring into being, and become the person you were originally created to be. You are a powerful, anointed being who is made in His image and His likeness.

> I am convinced that any suffering we endure is less than nothing compared to the magnitude of glory that is about to be unveiled within us. The entire universe is standing on tiptoe, yearning to see the unveiling of God's glorious sons and daughters! (Romans 8:18–19 TPT)

www.ingramcontent.com/pod-product-compliance
Lightning Source LLC
Chambersburg PA
CBHW022014160426
43197CB00007B/425